BEVERAGE CONTAINERS

RE-USE OR RECYCLING

ORGANISATION FOR ECONOMIC
CO-OPERATION AND DEVELOPMENT

The Organisation for Economic Co-operation and Development (OECD) was set up under a Convention signed in Paris on 14th December 1960, which provides that the OECD shall promote policies designed:
- to achieve the highest sustainable economic growth and employment and a rising standard of living in Member countries, while maintaining financial stability, and thus to contribute to the development of the world economy;
- to contribute to sound economic expansion in Member as well as non-member countries in the process of economic development;
- to contribute to the expansion of world trade on a multilateral, non-discriminatory basis in accordance with international obligations.

The Members of OECD are Australia, Austria, Belgium, Canada, Denmark, Finland, France, the Federal Republic of Germany, Greece, Iceland, Ireland, Italy, Japan, Luxembourg, the Netherlands, New Zealand, Norway, Portugal, Spain, Sweden, Switzerland, Turkey, the United Kingdom and the United States.

∗∗∗

© OECD, 1978
Queries concerning permissions or translation rights should be addressed to:
Director of Information, OECD
2, rue André-Pascal, 75775 PARIS CEDEX 16, France.

FOREWORD

The quantities of waste to be disposed of have increased substantially in many areas over the last few years. Environmental considerations, especially air and water protection measures, as well as the scarcity of suitable tipping sites, have also contributed to make waste disposal much more difficult and expensive. Recognizing that waste should no longer be looked at from the sole disposal point of view, the OECD Environment Committee, through its Waste Management Policy Group, has already developed the principles of a comprehensive waste management policy: i.e. a coherent system of measures concerning the design, manufacture and use of products as well as the reclamation and disposal of waste, and aiming at the most efficient and economic reduction of the nuisances and costs generated by waste. These principles were embodied in a Recommendation adopted by the OECD Council in September 1976.

Because of its increasing predominance in the waste stream packaging has become the focus of a great deal of public and government attention in recent years. The present report considers the impacts of different beverage containers systems upon waste generation, resource use and the environment, and discusses the likely consequences of various policy options designed to cope with the adverse effects. It was drafted by Mr. Richard Grace and Mr. Jonathan Fisher, on the basis of information previously assembled by Mrs. Susan Spence, and finally adopted in October 1977 by the Waste Management Policy Group.

Based on the findings of this report a Recommendation on the reuse and recycling of beverage containers has been adopted by the OECD Council. The text of this Recommendation is reproduced as Appendix 4.

DEFINITION OF TERMS USED

<u>Returnable</u> is the general term used for a beverage container that is intended to be re-used or recycled.

<u>Refillable</u> is a specific term for a returnable that is designed to be re-used in its original form as a beverage container.

> Frequently the distinction between returnable and refillable is a matter of semantics, in which case the more general term returnable has been used in this report. However in certain circumstances the distinction is necessary, e.g. the metal can under mandatory deposit legislation is returnable but not refillable.

<u>System</u> - The term system is used to describe all processes relevant to a particular beverage container type, i.e. from raw material extraction to the final disposition by the consumer.

<u>Trippage</u> - The number of times a refillable bottle is used for delivering beverage to the consumer.

<u>Bimetallic can</u> - A can with an aluminium closure and a tinplated steel body and base.

<u>Industry</u> - Unless otherwise specified this term refers to trade and industry.

<u>Social costs</u> - Social costs are the total costs for an economic activity and comprise both internal and external costs (see SECTION 4.a for more details).

CONTENTS

I. INTRODUCTION AND SUMMARY 7

    a. Introduction 7
    b. Summary and Conclusions 9

Part I

II. HISTORICAL BACKGROUND TO THE BEVERAGE
CONTAINER ISSUE 19

    a. Beer and soft drinks 19
    b. Wines and spirits 25
    c. Milk 26
    d. Mineral Water 27
    e. Summary 27

III. INTERNAL SYSTEMS COST AND TRIPPAGE 30

    a. Internal Systems Cost 30
    b. Definition and Derivation of Trippage 36
    c. Current Trippage Rates 36
    d. Trends in total trippage 38

IV. EXTERNAL COSTS 40

    a. Conceptual framework 40
    b. Solid Waste Generation 43
    c. Litter 50
    d. Pollution 58
    e. Hygiene and Health Problems 64
    f. Energy and Materials Use 67

Part II

V. POLICY MEASURES 85

    a. General Criteria for Policy Selection 85

        5.a.1. Environmental Benefits 86
        5.a.2. Economic impact costs 88
            i) Determinants of Size of Economic Impact Costs 92
            ii) Determinants of Importance of Economic Impact Costs 93
            iii) Means to Alleviate the Adverse Economic Impacts 94
        5.a.3. Impact on the Government Sector 95
    b. Non-intervention 97
    c. Ban on all Non-refillable Containers 99
    d. Mandatory Deposits 100
    e. Oregon Type Legislation 108
    f. High Tax on Beverage Containers 110
    g. Product Charge on Packaging 113
    h. Low Litter Tax on Beverage Containers 115
    i. Standardisation and International Trade 118
    j. Recycling and Resource Recovery 122
    k. Technological Gains and Product Innovation 138

Appendix 1 - Calculation of Trippage 141

Appendix 2 - Role of Voluntary Cooperation 145

Appendix 3 - References 148

Appendix 4 - Recommendation of the OECD Council on the re-use and recycling of beverage containers 158

I

INTRODUCTION AND SUMMARY

INTRODUCTION

The objective of this report is to consider the impact of packaging systems upon resource use and the environment, by reference to a case study of beverage containers. Should these impacts be shown to be socially detrimental there may be justification for government intervention. Possible types of corrective government measures are discussed in terms of their likely success in dealing with any adverse impacts and the likely consequences of such measures in respect of other economic considerations such as employment, investment and consumer aspects.

<u>Type of Approach Used - the comparison of external costs and benefits</u>

The rationale for a cost benefit approach is that, generally, environmental goods (clean air, water, etc.) are not owned by identifiable members of the community and consequently are not bought and sold in an economic market as is usually the case with other goods. So it is unlikely that the consumption of environmental goods will be adjusted by economic considerations, this means that it is unlikely that environmental resources will be allocated in an optimal way unless there is intervention by the state. This occurs, quite simply, because in the absence of an economic market the cost of using environmental resources is zero even though they have a positive value; this in turn will lead to a level of consumption that is higher than is optimally desirable because the cost of that consumption is set too low.

Cost-benefit analysis is designed to consider these non-market goods such that government decisions may be taken so as to achieve a socially optimal allocation of all resources. Essentially, an attempt is made to identify all the costs and benefits, including the non-market costs and benefits, of a given policy. Frequently, the <u>private</u> costs and benefits may be ignored if it is felt that the economic market is efficient in its allocation of resources (i.e. in the absence of market imperfections); thus an estimate of the effects of a policy may be determined by a consideration of the <u>external</u> costs and benefits alone.

The impact of a move towards non-returnable beverage containers, for example, may incur costs in terms of environmental degradation;

these costs will not be reflected in economic markets and it becomes necessary to use a cost-benefit framework in order to establish the importance of these environmental impacts to determine whether or not there is a justification for government intervention.

For the reasons outlined above the analysis of this report is predominantly concerned with <u>external</u> costs.

Limitations of the Report

The scope of this study is very general and covers not only a wide variety of materials for containers but also a wide variety of containers for the various types of beverages. The materials covered include: glass, steel, aluminium, plastic and paper. The types of beverages covered include: soft drinks, beer, wines and spirits, mineral water and milk. It has been impossible to establish data for all combinations of beverage containers for all countries in the form required but, where available, all relevant information has been included. The most well documented area in the literature covers the relative merits of the glass bottle, in returnable and non-returnable form, and the metal can for both beer and soft drinks, thus the predominance in the discussion of this area.

Because of the variation in the types of products there are a great variety of factors which affect the type of container used. Consumption patterns and distribution networks will vary for different products and therefore caution should be exercised when comparisons are made between the various container systems. Similarly, the economic and social differences between countries will blur any direct comparison or recommendations based upon the experience of one country for implementation in another. In order to overcome these difficulties the experience for as many products and countries as possible has been included; where a similar trend or situation occurs this has been reported.

The Layout of the Report

The report is divided into two parts. Part I attempts to identify the impacts of the various container systems upon the environment. This is achieved through a discussion of the relevant external costs imposed by beverage containers: Solid Waste Generation, Litter, Pollution, Hygiene and health problems, Energy Use (Section 4).

Discussion of these aspects is preceeded by a section on Internal Systems Cost and Trippage (Section 3). Trippage, the number of times a returnable container is used, is a fundamental variable in any comparison of various container systems. So as to avoid any misunderstanding or confusion over this issue this section has been included at an early stage of the report.

The historical background of beverage containers is also considered in this part of the report (Section 2).

Part II of the report assesses the various government measures that may deal with the environmental impacts (Section 5, b-k) reported in Part I. The measures discussed include:

No action.
Ban of all non-refillable containers.
Mandatory deposits on all containers.
Oregon Type legislation.
High medium tax on all beverage containers.
Product charge on packaging.
Low litter tax on all beverage containers.
Standardization of Containers.
Recycling and resource recovery.
Technological gains and product innovation.

The approach used for evaluating the impacts of each of these policy measures is explained in Section 5.a. This section may be treated as a general method for policy evaluation of beverage container related legislation.

SUMMARY AND CONCLUSIONS

Historical background of beverage containers (Section 2)

This section is intended to give the status quo and likely trends of the beverage container market. Competition between the returnable and non-returnable beverage container may be seen by comparing the market shares of the alternative systems. As was stated above it is necessary to consider each product for each country separately. The data for beer and soft drinks in the USA and UK shows a strong positive trend towards non-returnable containers. Although no data is given the same trend is reported in Australia and similarly in Canada for soft drinks.

The major reasons for these trends are generally attributed to the following:

Increased distribution distances due to large scale bottling and canning plants.

Decreases in the relative price advantage of the returnable bottle over non-returnable containers.

Increasing relative costs of labour to materials and capital.

Increasing reluctance on the part of retailers to distribute beverages in returnable bottles.

Increases in consumer preference for convenience and other attributes of the non-returnable container.

It would appear at present that unconstrained market forces generate a steady move towards the use of non-returnable beverage containers. The experience of most countries suggests that any increase in the market share of the returnable container will only come about through government intervention of one form or another. This trend should be used as a backdrop when consideration of the present impacts of beverage container use is undertaken.

Internal Systems Cost and Trippage (Section 3)

A comparison of the internal costs of alternative beverage containers systems is given in this section. It is clear that the number of trips made by a returnable bottle is fundamental in establishing both the internal and external costs of these systems. Appendix 1 refers to this section and gives details on the construction of a trippage value. The fundamental relevance of trippage is emphasized at this stage of the report because it is such an important variable throughout the remainder of the study.

The major determinants of trippage are found to be:
- The increasing value of consumer convenience.
- The ease of return. (This will be a function of the degree of standardization and the number of retailers prepared to accept the returned bottle).
- The proportion of 'on' premise to 'off' premise sales of beverage containers.
- The size of the deposit (where applicable).

Solid Waste Generation (Section 4b)

Solid waste generation may be included as an external cost where the pricing mechanism for solid waste is indirectly levied. Generally, this will occur when solid waste disposal is undertaken by a municipality and paid for out of taxes; in this instance the impact of a product upon the waste stream (hence the environment) is not taken into account by either the producer or consumer in their purchasing decisions.

Consequently, it is necessary to identify the impact of different beverage container systems upon the solid waste stream. The impact ranking, in order of least waste generating first, is as follows:

- Returnable Glass Bottles (trippage 1.2 - 4).
- Cans.
- Non-returnable Glass Bottles.

It should be noted that where the ancillary packaging for returnable containers is not itself returnable this may lead to greater solid waste impacts. Though generally in most countries ancillary packaging (usually the plastic crate) is returnable, there are exceptions which may change the ranking shown above.

Flexible plastic and paper cartons may rank above returnable glass bottles for those beverages where such packages are suitable (non-carbonated beverages).

The quantity of beverage related solid waste varies between countries from 2 - 12% of all domestic solid waste; a move to a returnable system would generate benefits through a decrease in solid waste.

Litter (Section 4c)

Concern has been expressed by most countries over the external costs imposed by littering. In this respect it is necessary to consider the beverage containers' contribution to this problem.

Beverage containers may be identified as one of the largest product types in litter. On a unit count basis, beverage containers account for 7 - 30% of total littered items. However, this measure likely understates the true impact of beverage containers in litter because bottles and cans have a greater visual impact than the average piece of litter. Furthermore, their non-biodegradable nature suggests that they incur a cumulative effect if the litter is not removed. On a volume or weight basis, beverage container litter accounts for some 35 - 70% of all litter in the USA. At present there would appear to be no European data for weight or volume based surveys.

It was consistently found that the metal can has the highest probability of being littered. Next, followed the non-returnable bottle, and the refillable bottle had the smallest impact. Hence a move towards a returnable system would create favourable improvements upon the environment.

Pollution (Section 4d)

One of the greatest problems of estimating air and water pollution impacts is the difficulty in assessing the effects of various types of emissions. The quantity of emissions from the various container systems may be determined but this does not necessarily give any indication of the impacts of such pollution. Ideally a system of weighting is required in order that the impacts of a given quantity of various emitted substances may be compared.

Air pollution impacts of the various container systems give the following ranking, least polluting first:

- Returnable Container.
- Metal Can.
- Non-returnable Container.

The ranking for water pollution is similar:

- Returnable bottle.
- Metal Can.
- Non-returnable bottle.

However, this ranking depends critically upon trippage. In order for this ranking to be maintained the returnable bottle must achieve a trippage of 5 in the case of air pollution and more than 10 in the case of water pollution. Otherwise the returnable bottle may cause greater pollution than returnable containers.

The pollution problem caused by the beverage container is probably better solved by a national pollution control programme since it is unlikely that beverage container pollution itself is a significant enough proportion of total national pollution to justify intervention in the beverage container market on these grounds alone.

Hygiene and Health Problems (Section 4e)

There is no evidence to support the hypothesis that returnable bottles are greater risks to hygiene and health than non-returnable containers. Strict food regulations in most countries have ensured that the cleanliness of all containers is of a sufficiently high standard.

Energy Use (Section 4f)

The analysis of energy use provides the following ranking order, from least energy intensive to most energy intensive:

- Refillable glass and plastic bottles
- Non-refillable plastic bottle
- Bi-metallic can
- Non-refillable glass bottle
- Aluminium can.

This assumes that all containers are produced from virgin materials.

Flexible plastics and paper cartons may rank above returnable glass bottles for those beverages where such packages are suitable (non-carbonated beverages).

In order that refillable bottles achieve energy savings they must have a trippage of between 1 - 4 for beer and soft drinks and 3 - 10 for milk. Generally, these trippage figures are obtainable and so it may be concluded that a move towards a greater market share for refillable containers will result in energy savings.

In summary, the returnable beverage container system will in most cases generate lower external costs than the non-returnable containers. Obviously, this statement is dependent upon trippage but in all the areas considered, with the possible exception of water pollution, this trippage is achieved in most countries. However, the most significant of these external costs are litter and solid waste. Consideration of government intervention must therefore be primarily concerned with these two areas.

Part II - Policy Measures

In Part II of the report the likely impacts of a variety of government policy options designed to cope with environmental effects of the beverage container are considered.

Because of the uniqueness of the beverage container industry in each country it is impossible to recommend a specific policy that all countries should follow. Instead, included in Part II is a section (5a) which attempts to formulate a general criteria for policy selection which highlights the critical determinants of the various policies, costs and benefits. This will, it is hoped, enable individual countries to select that policy which produces the greatest social gain for their particular set of circumstances.

Any government intervention into the beverage container market will lead, at least to some extent, to dislocation impacts on the industry. Obviously these will vary from policy to policy and it is important that this is taken into account when formulating a policy. In this respect policies that may be phased in over a period of time will help reduce these impacts.

1. Non-intervention Policy (Section 5b)

This is the situation that will occur through normal market forces in the absence of government intervention. Generally it has been observed that the market share of non-returnables will increase and the trippage of returnable containers will fall. These two factors will lead to greater adverse environmental impacts. This is the baseline with which all other policies should be compared.

2. Ban on non-refillable containers (Section 5c)

A ban on non-refillable containers constitutes one of the most simple policy options open to governments. Obviously, such a measure would remove non-refillable containers from the market and decrease in due course the environmental costs associated with beverage container use. It would not, however, guarantee that containers are returned. Moreover, the simplicity of this approach, while favourable for administrative reasons, also creates rigidity which is likely to incur large dislocation costs throughout the industry if a significant portion of sales are already in non-refillable containers.

3. Mandatory Deposits on Beverage Containers (Section 5d)

This policy requires that all containers carry a refundable deposit. In effect this will discourage the use of non-refillable containers because the deposit will discriminate against the convenience characteristics of the previously disposable container.

The special advantage of this policy is that the 'litter-bug', the instigator of a major external costs, will forfeit his deposit and directly bear the costs of his actions. This policy is likely to have a marked impact on the relative market shares of the various container systems and hence on solid waste. A further advantage over a ban is that this policy is more flexible, and that it will allow recycling of containers and the possibility of introducing new container types.

This policy will incur dislocation impacts which might be less severe than those of a ban.

4. Oregon type legislation (Section 5e)

Oregon type legislation is a combination of policies 2 and 3 above and has the advantages of both, while attempting to minimise the disadvantages. The ban would extend to 'pull tab' cans, and a mandatory deposit would be applied to all other beverage containers. This policy has met with a great degree of success in Oregon. The economic impacts of this type of legislation may be reduced by a suitable phasing in policy.

The ban on the pull tab can averts most of the problems encountered by mandatory deposits alone. Because of the low value of a returned 'pull tab' can there is a very great incentive for manufacturers and retailers to dissuade consumers to return them; this increases the difficulty of administering policy 3. In the case of a glass bottle it is worth while for the manufacturers to encourage return so long as the cost of a returned bottle (mandatory deposit refund + handling costs) is less than that of a new bottle.

5. High tax on all beverage containers (Section 5f)

This policy is designed to internalise the external costs of beverage container use. Tax would be paid on the purchase of a new container. The effects on the policy would then be brought about through normal economic market mechanisms. The tax would increase the relative price differential between new and used container, a distinct advantage to the refillable container. This would generate an increase in demand by producers and bottlers for returned containers. The flexibility of this policy makes it very attractive as the tax may be gradually phased in over a period of time, reducing the dislocation impacts that may be incurred.

6. Product Charges on packaging (Section 5g)

Product charges deal with a much wider perspective than just beverage containers, that is charges would cover all packaging products. This should prove an extremely effective method of internalising the external costs associated with solid waste disposal and should generate considerable increases in the levels of recycling.

7. Low litter tax (Section 5h)

Where earmarking of funds is permissible, a low litter tax policy may be adopted. Although this policy is unlikely to have any effect upon the relative market shares of the various container systems it would provide finance to fund litter clean ups and educational campaigns. This policy will have no impact upon solid waste.

8. Standardisation of containers (Section 5i)

Standardisation is likely to increase the efficiency and feasibility of refillable container systems, since it would act favourably on the willingness of retailers to supply refillable containers and would decrease the inconveniences suffered by consumers when returning containers. This measure would also ease the purchase of empty containers at their resource value, without using a deposit system. Standardisation would however limit the introduction of new container types.

9. Recycling (Section 5j)

Recycling of the materials of which the containers are made would reduce adverse environmental impacts, especially solid waste, of beverage containers. Since this policy does not entail any direct government intervention in the beverage market, it would not cause major economic dislocations in the beverage industry. It is however unlikely to be sufficient by itself to tackle the full extent of the other external costs, and would have no effect upon litter or the relative market share of the refillable container.

10. Encouragement to technical developments (Section 5k)

Research and technical development may result in beverage container systems or materials more compatible with the concerns of environmental protection. The encouragement to research would be a useful weapon, even if its effects are only indirect and at longer term.

11. Combination Policies

Although individual policies have been treated separately this should not be taken to imply that they cannot be used in combination. Clearly some policies are more relevant to certain external costs, therefore each individual country having identified its major external costs may select the combination of policies to deal with their particular problems.

PART I

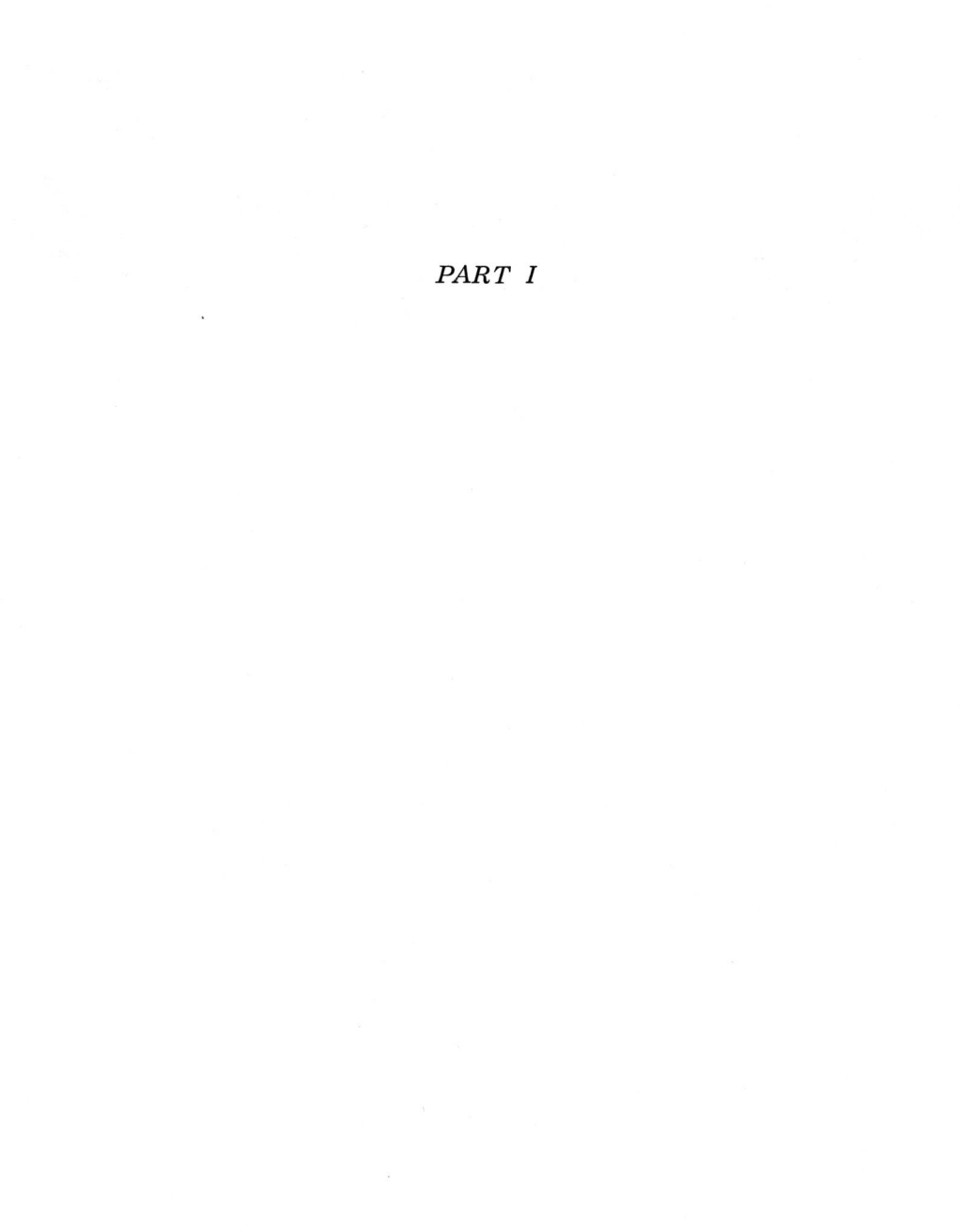

II

HISTORICAL BACKGROUND TO THE BEVERAGE CONTAINER ISSUE

It is becoming increasingly apparent that through the course of time the returnable beverage container is losing its share of the beverage container market to the 'throw away' convenience package.

It is necessary to assess this trend in the light of the likely environmental impacts that will be associated with such changes. This section attempts to show the extent and uniformity of this trend between countries for which data is available.

2. a. Beer and Soft Drinks

The trend is shown most clearly by the experience of the USA where the beverage market is dominated by beer and carbonated soft drinks. Tables 2.1 and 2.2 show for beer and soft drinks respectively

Table 2.1. BEER - BEVERAGE CONTAINER MARKET SHARE (%) USA
(Fillings of Packaged Beer)

	RETURNABLE GLASS BOTTLES	NON-RETURNABLE GLASS BOTTLES	METAL CANS
1963	46	16	38
1964	42	18	40
1965	41	19	40
1966	38	19	43
1967	35	21	44
1968	31	21	48
1969	29	22	49
1970	26	22	52
1971	23	21	56
1972	22	20	58
1973	19	21	60
(1975)*	(12)	(13)	(75)

SOURCE: US2.

* Forecast.

Table 2.2. SOFT DRINKS - BEVERAGE
CONTAINER MARKET SHARE (%) USA
(Fillings of Packaged Soft Drinks)

	RETURNABLE GLASS BOTTLES	NON-RETURNABLE GLASS BOTTLES	METAL CANS
1963	89	3.3	7.7
1964	86	3.6	10.0
1965	82	4.9	13
1966	75	7.9	17
1967	65	13	22
1968	58	15	27
1969	49	21	30
1970	40	27	33
1971	39	27	34
1972	38	28	34
1973	35	29	36
(1975)*	(25)	(21)	(54)

SOURCE: US2.

* Forecast.

the changes in market share over time for the metal can, the non-returnable and the returnable glass bottle.

Two trends are discernible from Tables 2.1 and 2.2. Firstly, it is clear that the change over from a returnable beverage container system to a non-returnable one has been very dramatic in both the beer and soft drinks market. Secondly, it is clear that the material used for beverage containers is rapidly changing from glass towards metals. The reasons generally given (US 2) for these trends are: increased distribution distances due to large scale bottling and canning plants; decrease in the relative price advantage of returnable bottles over non-returnable bottles and cans; increases in relative costs of labour to materials and capital; increases in retailers reluctance to distribute beverages in returnable bottles; and increases in consumer preferences for convenience and other attributes of non-returnable bottles and cans.

A very similar picture is emerging in the UK as regards the trend towards non-returnable beverage containers. Table 2.3 illustrates this trend. It shows clearly that the UK is beginning to experience precisely the same trends now clearly seen in the USA.

Table 2.3. BEER AND SOFT DRINKS
MARKET SHARE BY CONTAINER TYPE (%) UK
(Fillings of Packaged Products)

	RETURNABLE BOTTLES	NON-RETURNABLE BOTTLES	METAL CANS
1970	84	5	11
1971	81	6	13
1972	76	8	16
1973	73	9	18
1974	70	9	21
1975	66	10	24
(1979)*	(54)	(12)	(34)

SOURCE: Adapted from Metal Box Market Research Division (UK 17).

* Forecast.

The reasons for the switch to non-returnable are the same as those given for the USA, notably the reluctance of retailers to distribute returnable containers. This reluctance is due to increasing sales of beverage through supermarket retail outlets which boomed during the 1960's. Because of the supermarket's policy of low prices and fast turnover of goods, they have not been keen to promote the sales of returnable beverage containers and the consequent labour intensive collection process.

The Swedish experience during the last four years is somewhat different to that experienced by the UK and USA. Tables 2.4. and 2.5 summarise the changes in container market shares for these years.

Table 2.4. BEER
MARKET SHARE BY CONTAINER TYPE (%) SWEDEN*

	RETURNABLE BOTTLES	NON-RETURNABLE BOTTLES	METAL CANS
1972	57	9	34
1973	60.5	5.5	34
1974	58.2	3.3	38.5
1975	54.3	2.2	43.5

SOURCE: SWE 6.

* Class III (export) beer has been omitted.

Table 2.5. SOFT DRINKS
MARKET SHARE BY CONTAINER TYPE (%) SWEDEN

	RETURNABLE BOTTLES	NON-RETURNABLE BOTTLES	METAL CANS
1972	76	23	-
1973	79	21	-
1974	84	16	-
1975	91	8	1

SOURCE: SWE 6.

The obvious difference between the experience of Sweden and that of the USA and UK is the declining growth rate of non-returnable glass bottles. This is due to the impact of legislation in 1973, which taxed all returnable and non-returnable beverage containers, resulting in higher prices for non-returnables and larger deposits for returnables. The overall effect was therefore a relative price increase of non-returnable bottles to returnable bottles. However, it is noticeable that the switch from glass to metals in the beer market is in accordance with the USA and UK experience.

It is perhaps worth noting at this stage that it is important when comparing time series data between countries to separate out market effects and external effects which are generally created by government. The case of the USA and the UK are interesting because the lack of legislation gives a clear idea of the way in which market forces tend to operate in the beverage container industry.

It has not been possible to establish time series data for market share by container type for other countries but it would seem that the trends outlined above are broadly consistent throughout these countries where government intervention has been non-existent or of minor importance.

In Ontario it is reported (CAN 1) that the incidence of non-returnable bottles and metal cans has greatly increased in the soft drinks market, particularly during the 1960's. Beer sales, however, have been largely unaffected and remain predominantly in returnable bottles, due largely to an efficient distribution system operated by the breweries. Similarly, in Australia a clear trend towards throw away containers at the expense of returnable glass containers is described for beer and soft drinks (AUS 1).

The situation is less clear for countries that have enacted legislation and a discussion of trends here is deferred to Section 5 where a fuller discussion of the impacts of government intervention is given.

Although time series data is not available for other countries it is possible to establish cross-section data which shows the market shares for beer and soft drinks for a wide variety of countries. This data is given in Tables 2.6 A and 2.6 B, and shows where different countries stand at the present time.

Table 2.6. A. BEER
MARKET SHARES BY CONTAINER TYPE

(Millions of Litres)

COUNTRY AND YEAR	REFILLABLE GLASS	% P	NON-REFILLABLE GLASS	% P	METAL	% P	TOTAL PACKAGED VOLUME P
Canada Ontario 1972	448	97.9	-	-	9.5	2.1	458
United Kingdom 1975	1,133	67.5	40	2.4	507	30.1	1,680
France 1975	1,498	76.6	450	23.0	7	0.4	1,955
Denmark 1975	591	96.9	-	-	19	3.1*	610
Sweden 1975	231	50.5	10	2.1	202	44.2	444** (458)
Netherlands 1975	714	98.5	-	-	11	1.5	725
United States 1973	4,500	20.0	3,370	15.0	14,620	65.0	22,490
Norway 1975	161	99.7	-	-	1	0.3	162
Switzerland 1975	349	94.9	17	4.8	1	0.2	368
Germany 1976	6,319	93.6	250	3.7	181	2.7	6,750***

SOURCE: UK 22 (based on data from UK Glass Manufacturers Federation), FRG 3.

* Denmark expects that there will be no longer any metal cans by 1982, due to voluntary agreement between the Danish breweries.
** In Sweden 14 millions of litres (i.e. 3.2% of total packaged volume) are in plastic.
*** The figures for Germany refer to the total production packaged in containers; out of these figures 40 million litres (0.6%) in non-refillable glass, and 66 million litres (1.0%) in cans, were exported.

Table 2.6.B. CARBONATED SOFT DRINKS BY CONTAINER TYPE

(Millions of Litres)

COUNTRY AND YEAR	RETURNABLE GLASS	% P	NON-RETURNABLE GLASS	% P	METAL	% P	PLASTICS	% P	TOTAL PACKAGED VOLUME P
Canada Ontario 1972	209	48.8	76	17.9	143	33.3	-	-	428
United Kingdom 1975	1,051	62.9	241	14.1	370	22.0	9	0.6	1,671
France 1975	1,372	85.9	218	13.6	-	-	8	0.5	1,598
Germany 1976	3,662	88.1	204	4.9	290	7.0	-	-	4,156
Denmark** 1975	238	99.2	2	0.8	-	-	-	-	240
Sweden 1975	255	88	32	11.0	3	1.0	-	-	290
Netherlands 1975	722	94.8	-	-	16	2.1	24	3.1	762
United States 1975	8,168	38.0	4,729	22.0	8,598	40.0	-	-	21,495
Switzerland 1970	424*	100.0	-	-	-	-	-	-	424*

SOURCE: UK 22 (based on data from UK Glass Manufacturers Federation) - SWE 2 - FRG 3.

* Including mineral waters.
** In Denmark, by statutory order, effective June 1st 1977, the use of non-returnables for soft drinks has been prohibited.

Beer and soft drinks, however, do not encompass the entire beverage container problem, particularly in certain European countries where beverage consumption patterns are varied. It is important therefore that the beverage markets for milk, wines and spirits, and mineral waters are also considered.

2.b. Wines and Spirits

Generally, wines and spirits are treated together because separate data is not available. This does not present any great problem unless the consumption of either type of beverage is large. This would apply in the case of France in particular.

Time series data for market shares are not available for wines and spirits and therefore it is only possible to document the cross-section data from various countries. This is presented in Table 2.7.

It is quite clear from Table 2.7 that the non-returnable system for wines and spirits is very much more in evidence than for beer and soft drinks where returnable systems predominate. This is largely due to the specific market structure of the distribution industry for a particular country. Essentially in the case of Sweden (as in Finland and Norway) the existence of a refillable bottle system is due to the fact that wine and spirit stores are wholly state owned. Problems of buying back more bottles than were sold cannot, therefore, occur. In Denmark one supermarket chain buys back its own bottles from consumers.

Table 2.7. WINES AND SPIRITS
MARKET SHARE BY BEVERAGE CONTAINER SYSTEM (%)

	RETURNABLE	NON-RETURNABLE
Ontario, Canada	0	100
United Kingdom	0	100
United States	0	100
Netherlands	0	100
Germany	28.0	72.0
France	52.3	47.7
Sweden	71.8	28.2
Denmark	28	72

SOURCE: UK 22, SWE 5, DK 1, FRG 3, FR 2.

France presents a unique case because the consumption of wine represents a much greater share of the beverage market as a whole than in any other country. It is perhaps more enlightening to consider

the French wine market separately from the spirit market because
it represents a much larger industry in terms of quantity. A distinction
must be made between ordinary wine and fine wine due to the variation
of packaging between these two products. Most of the ordinary wines
(72% or 2,578 million litres) were packaged in returnable glass bottles
in 1975. A further 970 million litres were packaged in PVC containers,
and it seems that the trend towards PVC would increase in the future,
at least for ordinary wines. Fine wines, however, are predominantly
in non-returnable glass bottles (87%) and the extended trend is estimated
to increase to 91% by 1980 (EEC 1). Table 2.7 A also shows the data
for wine only.

Table 2.7. A. WINE
MARKET SHARE OF BEVERAGE CONTAINER SYSTEM

	RETURNABLE BOTTLE	NON-RETURNABLE BOTTLE (GLASS)	NON-RETURNABLE (PLASTIC)
France	77.7	14.5	7.8
Germany	44	56	0
Netherlands	0	100	0
Sweden	73	27	0
Switzerland	50	50	0
United Kingdom	0	99.4	0.6
Norway	74	26	0

SOURCE: FRG 3, UK 3, SWI 5, FR 2.

The predominant position of the non-returnable bottle in wines and
spirits can be explained by reference to three particular factors. Firstly,
the cost of the bottle as a percentage of the total product price is relatively small. Therefore it is unlikely that the effect of a deposit will
be very large. Secondly, due to the wide variety of wines and spirits
it is difficult to establish an economically viable system to return the
bottles to the original bottler where trade is carried out in bottled beverages. Thirdly, in most countries, the incidence of wines and spirits
sales is rather small compared to that of other beverages and re-use
would not benefit from collection economies that are available to other
more common beverage containers.

2.c. Milk

There is a trend towards non-returnable milk containers in many
countries. Data is not generally available but it is reported by Australia,

Denmark, France and the USA that this is the case. The trend is towards either plastic or waterproofed paper non-returnable containers, of which there are a wide variety due to the rapid technological advances that are occurring in the relevant industries.

In Ontario, in 1972, the returnable glass bottle accounted for 3.2% (CAN 1) of the total milk container market; this is a dramatic decline from the position in 1948 when returnable glass was the only container for milk. The market is now composed of a variety of containers, with the returnable plastic jug representing just under 50% of the market.
A ban has been implemented in Ontario to prevent the use of a 3 quart non-returnable plastic jug - a direct competitor to the returnable system.

The UK experience is markedly different to most other countries because the returnable glass bottle is still the predominant milk container. This is a direct result of the distribution method, where the vendor makes door to door deliveries and collections. It is the decline of this marketing system in many countries that has permitted the upsurge in non-returnable containers. The impact of supermarkets has also contributed towards the success of the non-returnable container for the reasons outlined above.

The main advantages of plastic and paper containers for milk are their lightness and resistance to light penetration.

Table 2.8 shows the market shares of various milk container systems for various countries where data is available.

2.d.   Mineral Water

Documentation and data for the consumption and container types for mineral water is very scarce. Table 2.9 summarises the data for France and Germany.

Mineral water is generally packaged in PVC containers in France, particularly for non-carbonated mineral water. Carbonated mineral water is packaged in roughly equal quantities of returnable and non-returnable containers.

Due to the lack of data from other countries it is not possible to report further upon the average container problem as it refers to mineral waters.

2.e.   Summary

Although it is impossible to consider the experience of all countries with regard to trends in beverage container market shares, it can be reasonably asserted that trends are bounded between at one extreme the maintenance of the status quo, that is where present container market shares remain constant (e.g. Canadian beer and UK milk) and at the other extreme a convergence towards a complete one way, throw away beverage container system. There has been no evidence from any country to suggest that the growth of a returnable system will be generated internally by unconstrained market forces; this will only be achieved by government action should it be found to be preferable.

Table 2.8. MILK
MARKET SHARES BY CONTAINER TYPE

(Million of Litres)

COUNTRY AND YEAR	RETURNABLE GLASS	% P	NON-RETURNABLE GLASS	% P	PLASTIC	% P	PAPER	% P	OTHER PACKAGED	% P
Ontario 1972	25.2	3.4	–	–	71.4	9.5	298.9	39.7	356.3*	47.4
United Kingdom 1975	6,670	91.3	–	–	636			8.7%		
Netherlands 1973	730	54.0								
France 1975	45	1.7	48	1.8	1,343	51	1,196	45.5		
Denmark	–	70.5	–	–	33.7	5.0	639.4	95.0		
Japan 1974	2,150	70.5	–	–	–	–	899	29.5		
Switzerland 1970	–	–	–	–	–	–	322	100		
Germany 1973	108	38	97	3.4	2,628			92.8%		

% P. Percentage of Total Packaged Milk Sold. (not draught).

*   Returnable plastic jug.

SOURCE: UK 22, DK 1, CAN 1, SWI 1, EEC 1, UK 25, FRG 3.

28

Table 2.9. MINERAL WATER
MARKET SHARE OF CONTAINER TYPE (%)

	RETURNABLE GLASS	NON-RETURNABLE GLASS	PLASTIC
France	14.5	5.5	80.0
Germany	95.0	1.0	4.0

SOURCE: EEC 1, FRG 3, FR 2.

There is a striking similarity of these trends between countries, although there are notable specific exceptions (e.g. Canada and UK noted above). It is clear that market forces tend to generate a move towards a non-returnable container system.

Differences generally occur between countries as to the type of non-returnable system that evolves. The metal can is generally the most predominant but there are also steady trends towards plastics, non-returnable glass and, in the case of milk, wax-coated paper.

III

INTERNAL SYSTEMS COSTS AND TRIPPAGE

3. a. Internal Costs of Alternative Beverage Container Systems

Table 3.1 shows the internal costs broken down into different items for three alternative container systems for soft drinks using 1972 data. These figures show the wholesale cost of soft drinks in the alternative containers. Retailing costs for the returnable bottles are generally higher than for non-returnable containers. Nevertheless recent studies (CAN 1, AUS 1, US 17, US 38) comparing the price and full internal cost to the consumer of beer, soft drinks, and milk in the various containers show the returnable to be still the cheapest container at the retail level.

It has been mentioned (Neth 10) that the US data in Table 3.1 may not accord with the european situation on account, in particular, of the use in Europe of a lighter, two piece can. Therefore Table 3.2 was drawn up which shows a cost comparison of returnable and non-returnable container systems for two European countries (Germany and Denmark). A similarly favourable position for the returnable system is apparent in a Dutch study (Neth 6). The Dutch study shows the returnable system to result in savings for the bottler of 34.13 Dutch cents per litre of beverage while incurring extra transport, wholesale and retail costs totalling 9.13 Dutch cents per litre so that overall the returnable system is 25.0 cents cheaper than the non-returnable container. The study assumes a trippage of 23. Thus, despite the special situation in Europe the returnable bottle is still the cheapest of the alternatives.

The important point to note in Table 3.1 is the different composition of the total internal costs for each container between the various cost items. The non-returnable containers, especially the can, have lower manufacturing costs due to greater speeds on the filling production line, and lower handling and storage requirements. The returnable containers incur greater distribution costs on account of the greater weight of the bottle and the return process. However, these extra costs of the returnable system have to be balanced against the savings in container costs. These container cost savings depend on the number of trips achieved by the returnable bottle as can be seen by comparing colums 1 and 2 in Table 3.1, and graphically in Fig. 3.1.

Table 3.1. COMPARATIVE STANDARD COSTS PER CASE
(24 x 12 oz. CONTAINERS)
OF RETURNABLE AND NON-RETURNABLE BOTTLES
AND METAL CANS FOR SOFT DRINKS

Container systems costs per case

COST ITEM	RETURNABLE BOTTLE TRIPPAGE = 1*	RETURNABLE BOTTLE TRIPPAGE = 23	NON-RETURNABLE BOTTLE	METAL CAN
Container Cost	$2.55	$0.11	$0.90	$1.08
Ingredients Manufacturing and Warehousing	0.60	0.60	0.50	0.45
Crowns	0.04	0.04	0.04	-
Packaging**	0.12	0.12	0.13	0.13
Delivery	0.50	0.50	0.33	0.29
Sorting and Handling Returns	0	0.18	-	-
AVg Cost per case	$3.81	$1.55	$1.90	$1.95
Margin/case		1.10	1.35	1.40
Wholesale Price/case		2.65	3.25	3.35

SOURCE: (US 17).

* Trippage is defined as the number of times that a returnable bottle is used for refilling and redelivering beverages.
** The packaging for the 23 trip returnable bottle is a returnable carrier with an assumed trippage of 2.2. trips.

Table 3.2. INTERNAL COSTS COMPARISON OF ALTERNATIVE CONTAINER SYSTEMS IN EUROPE

(A) Germany 1974 - DM per 1,000 litres of beverage

	BEER			SOFT DRINKS		
	BOTTLE		METAL CAN	BOTTLE		METAL CAN
COST ITEM	RETURNABLE[1]	NON-RETURNABLE				
Container	22.7	233.1	362.4	22.3	231.7	362.0
Packaging	4.0[2]	212.5	55.0	4.0[2]	55.0	55.0
Return and Re-use	112.0	-	-	50.0	-	-
Difference from Returnable	138.7	445.6	417.4	76.3	286.7	417.4
		306.9	278.7		210.4	341.1

SOURCE: FRG 3.
NOTES:
1. The returnable beer and soft drinks bottle has a trippage of 15.
2. The packaging for the returnable bottles relates to re-usable plastic crates.

(B) Denmark - Ores per litre

	CONTAINER SYSTEM	
BEVERAGE	NON-RETURNABLE	RETURNABLE- 5 TRIP
Beer	127	100 (90[1])
Milk	178	63

SOURCE: DK 1.
NOTE: 1. 90 Ores per litre of beer is the total internal systems cost of a 33 trip returnable beer system.

32

Figure 3.1

A COMPARISON OF THE TOTAL INTERNAL COST
OF NON-RETURNABLE AND RETURNABLE CONTAINERS
FOR DIFFERENT TRIPPAGES

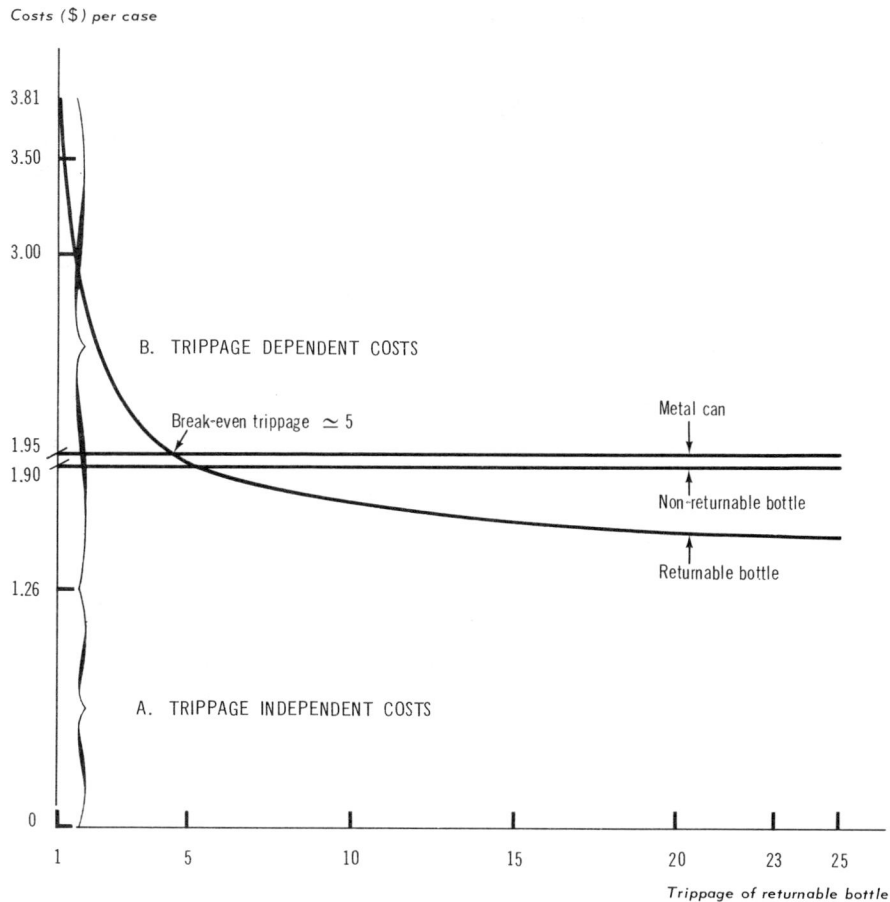

Source : Adapted from Table 3.1 (US 17).

In Fig. 3.1, (A) relates to the trippage independent costs of the returnable (C Ind) which are those costs that are incurred regardless of whether the bottle is returned. Such costs are the manufacturing, packaging, crowns and delivery costs; (B) relates to the unit costs that are dependent on trippage, which contains two elements; the costs of the actual bottle (CB) and the costs of returning the bottle for refilling (Cref). If the trippage independent costs plus this cost of returning the bottle are less than the total internal costs of the non-returnable bottles and cans (C_{NRB}), then the returnable bottle system will become an increasingly cheaper alternative as trippage increases and thus the trippage actually achieved is the essential determinant of the relative viability of the returnable system.

The breakeven trippage (T*), that the returnable must achieve in order to be viable, can be calculated to be nearly 5 from the figures in Table 3.1 by the use of the following formula:

$$C_{Ind} + \frac{CB}{T^*} + \frac{T^* - 1}{T^*} \times Cref = C_{NRB}$$

where the symbols are as defined above.

Estimates for cost breakeven trippages from other studies and sources range from 3 to 5 for beer and 5 to 7 for soft drinks (US 19, US 17, US 9).

The formula above shows that, in addition to trippage, four other variables will determine the relative internal costs and viability of the alternative container systems. These are the costs of the returnable bottle (C_B); the total costs of the non-returnable system (C_{NRB}), of which the cost of the actual container is the principal component; the trippage independent costs (C Ind); and the return costs (Cref) of the returnable bottle, which will largely be determined by the extra labour requirements and the transportation distances involved in the return process.

It will be evident in Section 4, when we consider the external costs imposed on society by the alternative container systems, that the social viability of the returnable bottle also depends crucially on the trippage achieved. Table 3.3 shows the breakeven trippage that the returnable bottle must attain in order to yield social benefits over the non-returnable containers in the form of lower energy consumption and solid waste generation.

The important external cost of litter is not included in Table 3.3, since the rate of littering does not directly depend on trippage. However, trippage will be dependent on litter to the extent that the littering of a returnable bottle is one of the possible leaks in the system that will prevent the bottle from being used again.

Thus trippage will play a central role in determining both the internal and external costs and benefits of the returnable bottle system; CAN 1 shows that 95% of the solid waste reductions caused by the Oregon Bottle Bill were due to the rise in trippage. Therefore it is necessary to consider trippage in detail.

Table 3.3. BREAKEVEN TRIPPAGE FIGURES FOR THE RETURNABLE GLASS BOTTLE IN COMPARISON WITH 6 ALTERNATIVE NON-RETURNABLE CONTAINERS WITH RESPECT TO ENERGY CONSUMPTION AND SOLID WASTE GENERATION

ALTERNATIVE NON-RETURNABLE CONTAINER	BEVERAGE	EXTERNAL COST		
		ENERGY	SOLID WASTE WEIGHT	SOLID WASTE VOLUME
Aluminium Can	Soft drink and beer	1-2	n/a	n/a
Bimetallic Can	Soft drink and beer	1.5-4	4-10	4
Glass Bottle	Soft drink and beer	1.5-2	1.5-2	1.2
Plastic (Rigello) Bottle	Beer	5-7	18	n/a
Plastic (PE) Bottle	Milk	10	n/a	n/a
Plastic Pouch	Milk	7-10	n/a	n/a
Paper carton	Milk	3-5	n/a	n/a

SOURCE: Table 4.31, CAN 1, SWE 4.

3.b. Definition and Derivation of Trippage

Trippage is defined as the number of times that a returnable bottle is used for filling and delivering beverages. Figure 3.2 shows two potential leakages to the beverage container system which will prevent a returnable bottle from being re-used.

Figure 3.2

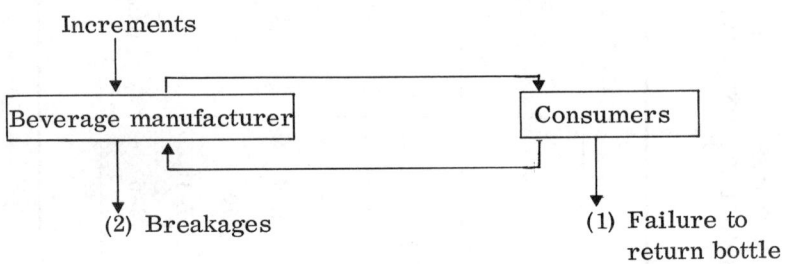

(2) Breakages   (1) Failure to return bottle

The first leakage relates to the consumers' average rate of returning bottles (ARR) rather than disposing of them in domestic waste or litter. This yields a consumer trippage (Tc).

The consumer trippage (Tc) is the number of times that returnables are returned. However, this will not equal the number of times that they are re-used on account of the second leakage (in-plant breakage APB) so that total trippage (T_T) is given by the formula below:

$$T_T = \frac{1}{1 - (ARR - APB)}$$

Estimates for the APB (in-plant breakage rate) range from 1% (CAN 1) to 2.1% (SWE 5) and 2.6% (DK 1).

Two similar methods (UK 1, SWE 5) have been developed for calculating total trippage (T_T); the formula for deriving total and 'off' premise trippage are given in detail in Appendix 1.

3.c. Current Trippage Data

Table 3.4 shows that for soft drinks, beer and milk the current total trippages achieved, in the countries shown, exceeded the break-even trippage figures in Section 3.a. However, the trippage data in Table 3.4 with the exception of the Ontario (CAN 1) and Oregon (US 4) data is an aggregate figure. Ideally the trippage data should be disaggregated into the separate and distinct beverage markets. Thus, it is useful to distinguish between 'on' premise and 'off' premise sales since they represent different beverage markets with different trippages. Trippage for returnables will be lower for 'off' premise than 'on' premise consumption since the 'on' premise system represents a closed circuit loop which facilitates return. It is necessary to evaluate 'off'

Table 3.4. CURRENT TOTAL TRIPPAGE DATA (T_T) OF RETURNABLE BOTTLES FOR BEER, SOFT DRINKS, MILK, WINE AND SPIRITS FOR 9 COUNTRIES

| YEAR | COUNTRY | CHARACTERISTIC OF BOTTLE OR MARKET | BEVERAGE ||||
			BEER	SOFT DRINKS	MILK	WINES AND SPIRITS
1974	UK		13.4	9.0**	26	–
1972	Ontario (Canada)	Total market	22	13	200*	–
		Urban Centre		5-7		–
–	Australia		6-7	12-30	45	–
–	Germany		25	9		–
–	Switzerland		60-80	20-70		30*
1975	USA	Total market	14	10		
	Oregon (USA)	Regional Brewers	7-10			
			20	$\overline{30}$		
				$\overline{17}$		
				$\overline{30}$		
1974	Denmark					1.15
1972	Sweden					1.6
1975	Finland					8

This refers to refillable plastic jugs.

This figure is an average of a wide range of actual trippages achieved.

SOURCES: AUS 1, CAN 1, DK 1, FIN 1, FRG 2, SWE 5, SWI 2, UK 1, UK 19, UK 21, US 2, US 4.

premise trippage to determine whether the returnable is socially preferable to the non-returnable in this market, especially since any policy will primarily be directed to the 'off' premise market. Unfortunately, the calculation of disaggregated trippage figures for the different beverage markets is a very difficult and frequently impossible task. It is for this reason that, when one moves from the ideal to the real world, most of the currently available trippage data relates to the aggregate beverage market and even this aggregate calculation is subject to some uncertainty, for reasons given in Appendix 1. In fact these uncertainties make it desirable to analyse in depth the calculations and assumptions behind the aggregate figures. Unfortunately, a shortage of the necessary information precluded such an analysis in this report. Appendix 1 contains the formula for deriving and calculating 'off' premise trippage. This highlights the severe information problems encountered in making such a calculation and it is generally agreed that the 'off' premise trippage is lower than the total trippage, but there is a lack of agreement and data on its actual size. The data we gathered shows estimates for soft drinks and beer varying from 3 to 13 with an average of about 6. This exceeds the breakeven trippage for the returnable bottle in comparison with the alternative containers for energy, and with the non-returnable bottle, but not the metal can, for solid waste (see Table 3.3). However, without more concrete data this remains a tentative conclusion and obviously the 'off' premise trippage will take on different values for each country depending on their different values for total trippage, 'on' premise trippage and the proportion of returnable sales in 'on' and 'off' premise consumption. The countries concerned should attempt to derive their own estimates for these parameters and then see if the resulting 'off' premise trippage exceeds the breakeven trippage.

3.d. Trends in total trippage

Table 3.5. based on a RTI study (US 2), shows that there has been a sharp decline in trippage during the last 20 years in America and a similar picture holds for UK (UK 21), although it has been brought to our attention that this decline in trippage is not apparent in Switzerland and Germany.

The RTI study made its forecast for declining trippage, in the 1980's, on the basis of projected rises in income levels increasing the value of time, which raises the inconvenience cost of returning returnables and increases the convenience value of the disposable containers. However, this argument is open to question since, if the return is made during the normal course of shopping, then no extra time is involved. The increasing inconvenience costs of return may be more due to the reduction in the number of retailers that accept returnable bottles, which has made it less easy for the consumer to return the bottle. This has accompanied the falling market share of the returnable bottle.

Table 3.5. THE TRENDS IN TOTAL TRIPPAGE (T_T)
FOR SOFT DRINKS IN USA 1947-1973

	YEAR	BEER	SOFT DRINKS
	1947	32	24
	1960	25	18
	1970	17	12
	1973	14.6	10
Forecast	1980	11	7
Forecast	1985	9.5	5.7

SOURCE: US 2.

Metal Box (UK 17) suggests that the trend to 'off' premise beverage consumption, instead of 'on' premise consumption, has been a principal cause of the decline in aggregate trippage since the 'off' premise trippage is lower.

Other possible causes are: the decline in the real value of the deposit due to inflation; the increased handling and transportation costs of operating a return system. This increase is due to rising labour costs and the increased centralization in the beverage industry which has led to greater transport distance between the bottler and retailer.

The marked divergence, shown in Table 3.4. between the trippages experienced in different countries and different beverages, suggests a potentially fruitful avenue for research into the determinants of trippage. The returnables trippage, and the means to increase it, is the central issue of the beverage container question. Therefore this research would be particularly valuable if it could effectively highlight the crucial determinants of trippage (i.e. are ease of return or level of deposit more important).

IV

EXTERNAL COSTS

4.a. <u>The Conceptual framework</u>

Before undertaking a social appraisal of the alternative beverage container systems and the current trend towards throw-away containers, it is important to make clear the essential distinction between internal and external costs and benefits.

The internal benefits of a container will be the benefits that are fully perceived by the consumer in making his consumption decision and the internal costs are those which the producers (manufacturer, distributor and retailer) will take into account in making their choice between alternative containers. The external costs and benefits of a beverage container will be the costs and benefits that the container system will impose on society as a whole and which the individual consumer and producer do not take into account in their production and consumption decisions.

The internal costs and benefits are well documented by the packaging industry (UK 9, NETH 6) and include such items as the benefits consumers obtain from the convenience value of throw-away non-returnable containers and the cost savings that a non-returnable container system generates in the form of economies of scale, reduced handling, storage and labour requirements; against which have to be offset the extra container costs of a non-returnable system (see Section 3.a.).

There can be no doubt as to the existence of these internal costs and benefits but the important point, in relation to a <u>social</u> appraisal of beverage containers, is that they will automatically be taken into account by market forces; the internal benefits to consumers raise demand and, along with the internal cost savings of a non-returnable system, have been the principal reasons for the move from returnable to non-returnable containers in these countries where there is no external regulation in the beverage market, as was seen in Section 2.

However, the question of whether a government should intervene in the beverage container market will require it to take a social view of the current beverage container system and trends and decide whether the current market mix between returnables and non-returnables, that the private market forces of internal costs and benefits generate, is the same as the market mix that evolves when both internal and external, or social, costs and benefits are taken into account. The intervention by the government would only be justified when the socially desirable container mix differs from the market generated container mix. When viewed in this light, it can be seen that the internal costs and benefits of the alternative beverage containers systems are inapplicable to the issue of government intervention since the internal costs and benefits occur on both sides of the equation being the determinants of the private market solution and, also being taken into account in the evaluation of the socially desirable container mix. The relevant policy variables are the external costs and benefits of the beverage container systems, since these will be the cause of any divergence between the private market container mix and the socially preferred container mix.

Thus the desirability of government intervention and, if so, in what direction (i.e. favour returnables, non-returnable bottles, cans or plastic containers), will depend upon an analysis of the external costs and benefits related to beverage distribution. These externalities can originate from two sources of market imperfection. The first concerns the issue of consumer sovereignty, or whether the consumers' decisions in the current market place yield a true representation of their preferences. Various sources (CAN 1, CAN 4, UK 26, UK 27) advocate that consumer sovereignty is no longer present in the current beverage market since the consumers do not have full information and freedom of choice in making their decisions. Thus they argue that the consumers' choice of a non-returnable does not necessarily constitute a consumer preference for non-returnables if this choice was not based on a free comparison of the merits of all alternative containers. The question of whether the consumers' freedom of choice is limited in the current market situation depends principally upon:

- i) the availability, in the various retail outlets, of beverages in all the alternative container types;
- ii) the retailers' policy on price labelling for beverages; i.e. separation of the price of beverage from the deposit on the bottle;
- iii) the comparative advertizing levels for beverages in returnable and non-returnables respectively, and the effect of this on consumer sovereignty;
- iv) problems that consumers encounter in returning bottles on account of retailers' policies towards accepting and redeeming deposits on returned bottles.

The Ontario reports (CAN 1, CAN 4) give some evidence that, in Ontario, advertising levels are higher for non-returnables and that there is a 'lack of ready and real availability' of soft drinks in returnable bottles in many retail outlets. This has resulted in the Ontario government proposing action on the four areas (i)-(iv) above; MRI (US 9) gives further data which supports this view. At present insufficient data is available and more detailed information is needed on the four factors indicated above in order to evaluate definitively for all countries this complex and emotive question of consumer sovereignty.

The second source of market imperfection is the external costs and benefits generated at each of the process stages of delivering beverages to the consumer. It is useful to split these external costs and benefits into two categories.

The category concerns the situations where the beverage container systems use resources or result in actions which are <u>unpriced</u> in the current market place. This category contains four elements:

The final disposal of the beverage container by the consumer into:
(1) solid waste (e.g. via dustbins) (SW), or
(2) litter (L)
(3) environmental pollution in the form of air and water pollution generated at each process stage (EP)
(4) public health and hygiene aspects (H).

The second category relates to the use of resources which are considered to be <u>underpriced</u> in the current market. It is commonly advocated that this category will include the beverage container's consumption of:

(5) energy (and perhaps other raw materials) (E).

The elements (1)-(4) in the first category should be weighted in a full national analysis at the social valuation (λ) of the damage caused by these externalities. However for the second category, the energy and raw materials used by the beverage industry are already priced internally at their current market prices. Therefore it is necessary to ensure that this internal element in the cost of this resource is not included in the social appraisal of external costs. The use of energy is only an external cost if there is a difference between the resource's current market price (P_e) and its social opportunity cost (λ_e) which is the value that society, present and future, places on this resource. It is this difference ($\lambda_e - P_e$) that should be used to weight the second category of external costs.

Thus the government should consider intervening in the beverage container market, to favour the returnable or non-returnable, depending upon whether:

$$SW_{rb}\lambda_{SW} + L_{rb}\lambda_L + EP_{rb}\lambda_{EP} + H_{rb}\lambda_H + E_{rb}(\lambda_e - P_e)$$
$$\gtreqless SW_{nrb}\lambda_{SW} + L_{nrb}\lambda_L + EP_{nrb}\lambda_{EP} + H_{nrb}\lambda_H + E_{nrb}(\lambda_e - P_e) \quad (1)$$

or if:

$$\underbrace{\lambda_{SW}(SW_{rb} - SW_{nrb})}_{(1)} + \underbrace{\lambda_L(L_{rb} - L_{nrb})}_{(2)} + \underbrace{\lambda_{EP}(EP_{rb} - EP_{nrb})}_{(3)}$$

$$+ \underbrace{\lambda_H(H_{rb} - H_{nrb})}_{(4)} + \underbrace{(\lambda_e - P_e)(E_{rb} - E_{nrb})}_{(5)} \lessgtr 0 \quad (2)$$

Where the symbols are as defined above

i.e.
- rb = returnable container system
- nrb = non-returnable container system
- L = Litter
- SW = Solid waste generation
- EP = Environmental pollution (air and water pollution)
- H = Hygiene and public health aspects
- E = Energy consumption
- λ_i = Social valuation of these externalities

More data is available on this second source of market imperfection and the impacts of the alternative container systems on the five elements (1)-(5) above will now be analysed in greater depth.

Finally it should be mentioned that if the comparison of the external costs and benefits, in equations (1) and (2), reveals one container system to be socially preferable, then this is only a preliminary condition for the government to <u>consider intervention</u> in the beverage container market to favour that container system. In order for actual intervention to be desirable, then these external costs must be sufficiently significant to ensure that the benefits of the policy cover its administrative and economic impacts and to warrant action in this particular field rather than the use of general steering measures to tackle the externalities (e.g. energy taxes, anti-litter campaigns, pollution control). These aspects are considered in Section 5 where a general framework is developed of the criteria that should be followed in formulating a beverage container policy and an evaluation is made of the various alternative policy measures.

4.b. Solid Waste and Beverage Containers

4.b.1. The conceptual problem

Solid waste collection and disposal incurs considerable costs upon local municipalities. Generally, waste is disposed of to landfill sites as this is usually the cheapest disposal option available. However, the supply of suitable sites is not unlimited, added to which the costs of solid waste management are rising and it is therefore important to consider ways in which the quantity of waste may be reduced.

This section attempts to identify the impact of beverage containers in solid waste in order to assess the possibility of reducing this burden, by first considering the effects of the external costs associated with waste disposal.

One of the salient features of the "Beverage Container" as a waste problem is the extent to which beverage containers impose costs upon society once their useful life to the consumer is over. There are two categories of costs which may be differentiated in this respect. Firstly, those costs which are completely unpriced in the market, which comprise air pollution – from incineration, where this is used as a disposal option, and the aesthetic losses associated with despoiliation of natural endowments – resulting from unsightly dumps or litter. Secondly, the impact of municipal waste disposal operations, because they are generally mandatory for health and hygiene reasons, tend to distort the efficient pricing of free market mechanisms, and hence incur costs. This concept requires careful consideration. In the event that each individual in a society was charged <u>directly</u> for his waste to be disposed of it is likely that littering would increase dramatically because the option to litter would incur only minor private costs, i.e. the costs perceived by the "litter bug" of seeing his own litter, whereas sanitary and controlled waste disposal would incur higher private costs, i.e. the charge made for the removal of waste. When a municipality takes over the waste disposal operation as a legal requirement the cost is passed into the individual through local taxation or rates by means of some average cost pricing mechanism, invariably decided upon for administrative ease.* Payment of this levy is enforced through law. However, this system removes any marginal cost to the individual for small increases in his waste generation. Consequently, if the individual increases his waste generation by say, 10%, the cost of collection and disposal of this extra quantity is charged to all individuals in the area of the particular municipality. Hence, the marginal cost of waste generation to the individual approaches zero when the number of people in the municipal area is large. In the case of beverage containers the cost of disposing of the item, once it has been used, does not therefore become a consideration in the purchasing decision. It may be concluded that, although individuals pay for waste disposal through taxes or rates, these costs are external to the decision to purchase a particular item. This argument also works in reverse. If an individual purchases only returnable containers and duly returns them after use he will reduce his waste generation, but the savings will accrue to the waste disposal agency, the municipality, and will be passed on to all the individuals in the area through lower taxes or rates, so the individual, whose actions created the saving does not benefit proportionally and the incentives to reduce waste disposal costs are removed. The result of this distortion will cause beverage containers to command a price that is lower than their true or socially adjusted price, and hence larger allocations of resources will be directed to these products than are socially optimal.

  This situation will hold unless there is government intervention but this can only be justified if the cost of intervention is less than the costs presently endured due to the misallocations described above.

  It is, therefore, necessary to assess the impacts of beverage containers in the solid waste stream, in those countries for which data is available.

   * This is not always the case, as for example in Germany, Sweden and Denmark, where the consumer may pay more if he requires additional waste capacity.

4.b.2. The impact of the beverage container on solid waste

Data for solid waste generation is not very precise because it is normally collected on a sampling basis. Furthermore, data on the quantity of beverage containers in solid waste is usually estimated from production data adjusted for littering and private collection. Waste generation may be measured in either weight or volume and both measures may be relevant to particular aspects of waste management. It is suggested in CAN 1 that volume is the more useful measure for solid waste because firstly, municipal compactor vehicles for the collection of waste are constrained by the volume of waste, not the weight, and secondly the volume of waste is likely to be more critical than weight at a landfill site. The greater the volume of waste the shorter the life of the landfill site. Unfortunately however, data on volume is not readily available and because it is easier to weigh waste this is the statistic usually provided. Beverage containers are not likely to be greatly reduced in volume by compacting techniques because of their strength and uncrushable nature and consequently the use of weight rather than volume is likely to understate the impact of beverage containers in solid waste.

Table 4.1. shows the quantity of materials (not just containers), that we are concerned with, as a percentage share of all solid waste. It is clear that the shares are not greatly dissimilar between countries. The greater usage of cans in USA and UK is noticeable and the relatively low incidence of glass in Norway which has a wholly returnable system for bottles is apparent.

Table 4.1. COMPOSITION OF MUNICIPAL WASTE* (ALL USES)
Percentage by Weight

	GLASS	METAL	PLASTIC
USA	9	9	3
UK	9	9	1
Sweden	10-12	4-8	4-8
Germany	15	4	2-3
Australia	14	7	1-8
France	8	4-8	2-6
Netherlands	10-15	3-4	4-6
Canada	8	8	2-6
Norway	6	4	8
Finland	8	5	5
Switzerland	8	4	3
Denmark	4-8	3-5	4-7
Spain	6	4	9-12

* i.e. households plus commercial establishments but excluding industry.

Table 4.2. shows the percentage weight of carbonated beverage containers in municipal solid waste. It is clear from this table that beverage containers may frequently be identified as a sizeable and important constituent of municipal solid waste, but in order to compare the impact of a particular beverage container system this data must be disaggregated.

Table 4.2. CARBONATED BEVERAGE CONTAINERS' SHARE OF MUNICIPAL SOLID WASTE

	% WEIGHT
USA	4-6
Denmark	1
Sweden	7
Canada	6.8
Netherlands	2.65
UK	2.0
Germany (including wines and spirits)	11.7

The waste generated by a particular beverage container system as a percentage of all beverage container waste does not necessarily give a meaningful statistic because the market shares of beverage container systems are not equal. Therefore, the waste generation of a beverage container system must be compared with the market share of that system. Essentially, if the impacts upon solid waste are equal for all systems the ratio of solid waste generation to market shares for each container system will equal unity; if however the impacts are not equal then a value below unity implies that the system is relatively better in waste disposal terms and vice versa if the ratio is greater than unity. Tables 4.3. to 4.5. give these ratios for USA, Canada and Denmark. Solid waste generation has been estimated by weight.

The data for Ontario and the USA shows that the non-returnable glass bottle is far more likely to increase the weight of solid waste than either the metal can or the returnable glass bottle. In Denmark where the non-returnable bottle is virtually non-existent the returnable bottle has the most adverse effect upon the weight of solid waste. However, the situation in Denmark results mainly from the inclusion of wine and spirit bottles as returnables. Technically wine and spirit bottles may be classified as returnable but the trippage rate is estimated at 1.15, and some 75-80% of these beverage containers are discarded after use. It is therefore extremely important to note the effect of trippage upon this ratio. Wine and spirit bottles account for 62% (by weight) of the beverage container waste in Denmark whereas their market share in terms of quantity of liquid is only 4.3%. Therefore,

Table 4.3. RATIOS OF SOLID WASTE GENERATION
TO MARKET SHARE
USA 1971

CONTAINER SYSTEM	RATIO: $\dfrac{\text{SOLID WASTE GENERATION BY WEIGHT}}{\text{MARKET SHARE}}$
Returnable Bottles	0.43
Non-returnable Bottles	2.32
Cans	0.72

SOURCE: Adapted from US 2 and US 3.

Table 4.4. RATIOS OF SOLID WASTE GENERATION
TO MARKET SHARE
ONTARIO, CANADA 1972

CONTAINER SYSTEM	RATIO: $\dfrac{\text{SOLID WASTE GENERATION BY WEIGHT}}{\text{MARKET SHARE}}$
Returnable Bottles	0.32
Non-returnable Bottles	3.71
Cans	0.96

SOURCE: Adapted from CAN 1.

Table 4.5. RATIOS OF SOLID WASTE GENERATION
TO MARKET SHARE
DENMARK 1974 (Beer)

CONTAINER SYSTEM	RATIO: $\dfrac{\text{SOLID WASTE GENERATION BY WEIGHT}}{\text{MARKET SHARE}}$
Returnable Bottles	< 0.80
Paper cartons	0.64
Cans	3.04

SOURCE: DK 1.

a ratio of approximately 11 can be established for these products. Indeed, if this category is separated from the remaining returnable bottles the ratio's are in line with the results from Canada and the USA (see Table 4.6). It should also be noted that the paper carton, as used for 95% of all milk sales in Denmark has a ratio well below 1 implying that the impact of this beverage container system upon the solid waste stream is very low. Though it should be pointed out that on a volume rather than weight basis this ratio would be considerably higher for cartons.

Table 4.6. IMPACT OF BEVERAGE CONTAINERS ON SOLID WASTE DENMARK

CONTAINER	RATIO
Returnable bottles	0.13
Cans	3.04
Cartons	0.64
Wine and Spirit Containers	11

SOURCE: DK 1.

It should be noted, however, that the ratio is found by dividing the percentage weight of beverage containers by their percentage market share. No account has been taken of the ancillary packaging which may accompany the various beverage containers. For example, most glass containers require packaging in cardboard boxes in order that they may be transported. Each bottle must be separated by dividing the package into sections. This packaging material is likely to increase the weight of solid waste. Metal cans and paper cartons, however, do not require such elaborate packaging because they are unbreakable. If the ancillary packaging is included the results will be altered. This data is given in Table 4.7 for the USA.

It can be seen that the packaging content for glass is large enough to alter the ranking of returnable glass containers from first to second position and metal cans move to first position. This may however be a soley American feature due to the predominance of one way ancillary packaging. In Denmark, for example, the use of a returnable crate with very high trippage leads to no increase in the quantity of solid waste when ancillary packaging is included.

Solid waste management is concerned with two distinct operations namely, collection and disposal. In order to assess the solid waste costs of beverage containers, these two operations should be treated separately.

Table 4.7. SUMMARY OF POST-CONSUMER SOLID WASTE GENERATION BY CONTAINER TYPE PER 1,000 GALLS-BEER/SOFT DRINKS UNITED STATES

	19 TRIP RETURNABLE BOTTLE	10 TRIP RETURNABLE BOTTLE	5 TRIP RETURNABLE BOTTLE	NON-RETURNABLE BOTTLE	STEEL CAN	ALUMINIUM CAN	PLASTIC BOTTLE STEEL CLOSURE
Post Consumer Solid Waste (cu.ft.)	7.16	11.96	28.88	40.87	3.22	2.75	27.05

SOURCE: US 6.

Collection is normally carried out by local municipalities at regular intervals; collection costs will be related to the frequency of collection, the distance between the collection points and the amount of waste generated. Because of the need for regular collections it is frequently the case that small changes in the quantity of solid waste generation will have little impact upon collection costs; while this is certainly true in the short run, it is not so clear that in the long run this conclusion will hold. It has been argued that if charges were made on products to account for the costs they incur on solid waste collection and disposal this would be inequitable, because collection costs would not fall in a linear relation with reductions in solid waste generation. However, this will always be the case if the product under scrutiny is small in relation to all solid waste. There are two ways to approach this problem: firstly if collection costs were re-allocated directly - product by product, the impact on solid waste is likely to be more than marginal - even though the impact of any one product would be small. Secondly, solid waste can be broken down into its major constituents and then policy may be directed towards these constituents. For example, packaging constitutes some 30%-60% of all commercial and domestic solid waste and a policy directed to packaging would undoubtedly have a more than marginal impact on solid waste; obviously any legislation directed towards packaging would encompass beverage containers.

Disposal costs are more directly related to the quantity of solid waste and therefore the allocation of average disposal costs, on a weight or volume basis, is generally straightforward. However, any reductions in solid waste will yield disposal cost savings which, in the short run at least, will be less than the average disposal costs on account of any fixed cost element of disposal costs.

The total cost of solid waste collection and disposal varies from country to country, but the proportion between collection and disposal is relatively constant and of the order of 70% and 30% respectively. Because collection costs are the major determinant of total cost it is important that these costs are not omitted in policy formulation simply because they are not linearly related with the quantity of solid waste.

Table 4.8 shows the comparison between costs of collection of 1,000 litres of packaging in glass (returnable and non-returnable), tinplate, paper carton and polyethylene (PE). The least costly to collect in the following order are PE, returnable bottle, paper carton, tinplate can and finally the non-returnable bottle.

It is clear from this section that plastics and paper cartons have very low impacts on solid waste but clearly these types of containers are only applicable to non-carbonated beverages. Returnable glass and metal cans are better than non-returnable glass containers which constitute the major impact. Returnable glass containers, however, are dependent upon high trippage figures if their relatively low impacts are to be maintained. It should also be stressed that much of these conclusions derive from impacts assessed by weight, whereas had it been possible to use volume the superiority of the returnable bottle may well be even greater. The relative merits of particular beverage container systems are not, however, the only consideration. Policies designed to reduce the incidence on non-returnable glass containers and cans are likely to produce savings in solid waste collection and disposal costs. This would appear to be an area in which benefits from beverage container legislation will be apparent.

4.c. Litter

It is felt (US 3, SWE 4, SWE 5) that the beverage container contributes significantly to the litter problem and it has been concern over this contribution that has been the principal motivation behind the proposal in America of 356 litter control bills dealing specifically with beverage containers (US 19), the most notable of which are the Oregon Bottle Bill and Washington Litter Tax. However, many of the European delegates have commented that in Europe the littering of beverage containers does not have the same predominance that is apparent in America with respect to the beverage container question. Thus, the other external impacts (e.g. solid waste) take on a greater significance.

It costs considerably more to collect litter than ordinary household solid waste. Estimates for litter collection and disposal costs range

Table 4.8. SENSITIVITY OF COLLECTION COSTS TO TYPE OF PACKAGING MATERIAL SOLID WASTE DISPOSAL COSTS PER 1,000 LITRES OF BEVERAGE CONTAINER (DM)

BEVERAGE	RETURNABLE BOTTLE (T = 15)	NON-RETURNABLE BOTTLE	TINPLATE CAN	PAPER CARTON	PLASTIC (NON-RETURNABLE) PE BOTTLE	PLASTIC (NON-RETURNABLE) PE POUCH
Beer	4.0	69.3	24.8	–	–	–
Soft Drink	4.0	28.1	24.8	–	–	–
Cordial	3.3	34.7	20.0	7	2.8	–
Milk	3.3	–	–	4.9	2.8	0.9

NOTES: Collection Costs = 75%
Disposal Costs = 25%

SOURCE: FRG 2.

from US ȼ 1.9 to 3.9 per littered container (US 3 - 1969 figures) US ȼ 3.8 (US 9) and US ȼ 11.3 (SWE 5 - 1975). Thus using the US EPA (US 3) figures the 2,200 million beverage containers discarded there in 1969 would cost $ 41.8 to 85.8 million (in 1969 terms) if they were all collected. However, not all discarded containers will be collected. A certain proportion will remain as litter for some length of time and impose non-pecuniary nuisance costs in the form of an aesthetic eyesore and the damage to human and wildlife caused by broken glass and discarded ring pulls from cans.

Surveys show that 86% of respondents considered litter to be a serious problem (US 3) and this concern can be expected to increase in the future as the demand for leisure and travel increases and unless something is done to prevent the forecast trends in packaging and increased mobility from resulting in increasing quantities of litter. Thus beverage related litter is forecast to increase at 8% p.a. so that EPA forecast littered beverage containers to rise to 3,900 million in 1976 which will cost $ 98 million to collect and dispose (US 3). These costs will be borne by all tax payers regardless of whether they litter or not and is thus considered unequitable since in effect the non-littering tax payer is subsidizing the litterers.

However, although litter is one area where the beverage container's impact may be significant, it is also the area where there is least agreement over the relevant data. Thus estimates for beverage container litter as a percentage of total litter vary from 7% to 70% as can be seen in Table 4.9.

Table 4.9. BEVERAGE CONTAINER LITTER AS % OF TOTAL LITTER

LITTER STUDY	SOURCE	MEASUREMENT BASE	%
UK	(UK 4)	Unit Count	7
Australia	(AUS 1)	Unit Count	8.5–12
Sweden 1	(SWE 5)	Unit Count	12
Sweden 2	(SWE 5)	Unit Count	20
Ontario Help 1	(CAN 1)	Unit Count	9
Ontario Help 2	(CAN 1)	Unit Count	33
KAB 1	(AUS 1)	Unit Count	32
KAB 2	(AUS 1)	Unit Count	20
EPA	(US 20)	Volume	54–70
Oregon	(US 4)	Volume	43
Vermont 1	(US 19)	Volume	34
Vermont 2	(US 19)	Volume	57
Ontario Sweep	(CAN 1)	Weight	37

NOTE: The Oregon and Vermont results relate to litter studies undertaken before beverage legislation was introduced.

These discrepancies will be caused by differences in the characteristics of the study areas and four factors relating to the methodologies used by the studies. These four factors are:
  i) measurement base;
  ii) definition of litter;
  iii) definition of beverage related litter;
  iv) frequency of litter data collection.

The principal cause is the different measurement bases used in the study. Beverage containers are larger and heavier than most litter and therefore will show up as bigger percentages of litter in a weight or volume measure than a unit item count measure. The use of a unit count method (one sweet wrapper = one can = one bedstead) is very common and advocated on the grounds that the costs of litter collection are determined more by the pieces of litter to be picked up than by volume or weight. However, the use of a volume measure is advocated on the grounds that it is a better surrogate for the visual impact of the litter. The ideal measure is one that reflects the external social cost of litter. This is difficult to achieve but the unit count measure probably reflects well the pecuniary collection costs of litter while understating the non-pecuniary nuisance costs of litter. This view is supported by the results of surveys which show that the public's impression of the contribution of beverage containers to total litter is much greater than the statistical figures (US 17). Therefore volume should be used as a measure of the nuisance cost, but even this will fail to take into account the extra injury problems of broken glass and ring pull tabs and the extra visual impact of a beverage container; this highlights an essential conflict between the beverage container's role of sales promotion in supermarkets and its position in litter.

The results will vary depending upon how total litter and beverage related litter is defined and how consistently it is applied. Thus does litter mean all articles found on the roadside or will only deliberately discarded items be included and will small items of litter be classified separately or in the large body of miscellaneous litter or not at all? Beverage related litter should encompass the beverage container (in its entirety or in pieces), its closure or ring pull and any supplementary packaging. Some of the difference, between the Ontario Help 1 and the Ontario Help 2 studies, can be accounted for by the fact that Help 2 included broken glass and closures while Help 1 did not.

Frequency of data collection. Beverage containers are more permanent than most items of litter since they do not biodegrade or blow away like paper. Therefore the percentage for beverage container litter will be higher when the collection of litter and litter data is less frequent. Thus the first Keep America Beautiful study (KAB_1) which represents the accumulated quantity of litter found in the first pick up, yields a larger percentage figure than the second litter pick up shown in the second (KAB_2) study which represents the rate of littering during the study period. This factor partly explains the low UK figure from the Glass Manufacturers Federation (UK 4) since the litter survey was taken very soon after the August Bank Holiday and also used an item count unit of measurement.

The percentage results will be greater for rural and minor roads than main highways due to the lower speed and frequencies of litter collection on the minor roads. This can be seen in Table 4.9 in the difference between the Vermont 1 study which relates to a 4 lane highway and the Vermont 2 study which relates to an urban road. The visual impact on minor roads could be expected to exceed that on fast highways. Most of the litter data relates to road litter whereas the bulk of the nuisance costs of litter will be incurred in beaches and public recreation areas; Stern (US 17) estimates that the beverage container accounts for 40-60% of this litter.

The rate of littering is determined by a number of variables which include traffic density and speeds, the levels of tourism, beverage consumption, the season and the effectiveness of any anti-litter programme. These variables will take on different values in different regions and different time periods and will therefore play a large part in explaining differences in inter-regional and intertemporal comparisons.

It is unfortunate that most of the data in Table 4.9 relates to American/Canadian experience. The reason for this is that, apart from the UK and Swedish surveys, most of the work on this subject has been undertaken in North America, since it is in North America that the beverage container litter problem is more pronounced. However further litter studies are currently being undertaken in the UK and the Netherlands. These studies should throw some much needed light on the question of the beverage containers' contribution to the litter problem in Europe.

4.c.1. The Alternative Beverage Containers in Litter

Column 1 in Table 4.10 shows the distribution of beverage container litter between non-returnable and returnable bottles and metal cans. Such data has provoked comments that the returnable bottle causes more litter than the non-returnable bottle. But such analysis, based solely on this data, is meaningless since what we are interested in is whether the sales of beverages in returnables creates more or less litter than the sale of beverages in non-returnable containers. Therefore we have added a second column for the distribution of beverage sales between the three container types and hence evaluated the Average Propensity of each beverage container to appear in Litter (APL); where APL is the number of that beverage container type found in the litter survey (Bi) divided by the total beverage sales in that container type (Si).

$$APL = \frac{Bi}{Si}$$

where i = container type, i.e. returnable, non-returnable, etc.

Table 4.10. THE DISTRIBUTION OF BEVERAGE LITTER AND BEVERAGE SALES BETWEEN THREE ALTERNATIVE CONTAINERS FOR UK

BEVERAGE CONTAINER	(1) No. FOUND IN LITTER SURVEY	(2) BEER AND SOFT DRINKS SALES (IN MILLIONS) IN EACH CONTAINER	APL (1) : (2)
Bottle returnable	138	6,849	0.02
Non-returnable	271	685	0.4
Metal Can	1,185	1,405	0.84

SOURCES: UK 4, UK 17.

APL's were also calculated for Australia, Canada, the United States and Sweden and are given in Table 4.11.

Table 4.11. AVERAGE PROPENSITY OF BEVERAGE CONTAINERS TO APPEAR IN LITTER (APL'S) IN 4 COUNTRIES

COUNTRY	BEVERAGE CONTAINERS' APL'S		
	RETURNABLE BOTTLE	NON-RETURNABLE BOTTLE	METAL CAN
Australia	0.68	1.8	5.9
USA	0.7	3.8	6.5
Canada (Ontario)			
Sweep Survey	0.14	0.22	1.7
Help Survey	0.17	0.2	0.8
Sweden	0.02	0.18	0.22

SOURCES: AUS 1, CAN 1, SWE 5, SWE 6, US 3.

The American and Australian data related to national estimates of the total number of littered beverage containers, which was compared with national beverage sales in each container type, to show that 6-7% of metal cans, 2-4% of non-returnable bottles and 0.7% of the returnable bottles used for beverages were littered. Unfortunately, the Swedish and Canadian data were in the form of each beverage container's share of total litter and the UK data related to only a small portion of beverage related litter. Therefore a similar percentage interpretation cannot be made of the Canadian, Swedish and UK APL figures. However, the relative APL's for the three containers can still be compared for the seven studies and this shows that metal cans are littered between 5 and 42 times as often as a returnable bottle and that non-returnable bottles are littered between 1.2 and 20 times as frequently as a returnable beverage bottle.

These results suggest that, as well as being a people problem, litter is also a product problem and that the convenience characteristics of the disposable one way containers, especially the cans, result in a greater littering of this type of container; while the incentive to return a returnable bottle will result in a lower littering rate for the returnable and the action of scavengers, picking up returnables to gain the deposit, will result in less returnables appearing in accumulated litter. This conclusion is supported by evidence in the UK litter survey (UK 4) that the deposit bearing beer bottle was less apparent in litter than the non-deposit returnable milk bottle. The product problem will be related to the people to the extent that the recent growth in disposable beverage containers have contributed to the growth in the disposable ethic of modern society which has been a principal cause of the current growth in littering.

4.c.2. Critical Appraisal of the APL Results

In view of the controversy over litter data and the range of relative APL results, it is worthwhile to analyse the APL results with respect to the problem areas of litter data which were mentioned earlier.

The APL results relate to unit counts of litter but the metal can and bottle occupy roughly the same volume so that the use of the more relevant volume measure should not alter the relative position.

The APL results, with the exception of Sweden, only consider entire bottles; they do not consider broken glass, closures and ring pulls for cans - important areas of concern. Their inclusion would probably raise the APL's for non-returnable and returnable bottles more than it would for metal cans and thus reduce the unfavourable position of the metal can but not by a great deal since the Swedish study, which did apportion broken glass between the bottles, results in an APL for cans 11 times larger than the APL for returnable bottles. Similarly, the UK study which also included broken glass shows the APL for cans to be very much greater than the returnable APL (by 42 times).

The Action of scavengers will mean that the littering rates of returnables will be greater than their appearance rate in accumulated litter and therefore the relative percentages of returnables in litter will decline as the time period, since their disposal, lengthens and the frequencies of litter collections diminish. The USA data relates to the second Keep America Beautiful litter pick up and the UK survey data was collected very soon after their disposal on the August Bank Holiday and therefore these two studies will overstate the APL's returnables.

The relative APL results will vary for different beverage distribution systems and for any government regulations concerning beverage containers. The purpose of this part of the study is to examine the external impact of the various beverage containers under free market conditions and then consider if government intervention is justified.
It was for this reason that 1972 data was used for Sweden so as to give a picture of the litter position prior to government intervention. In Ontario there is a return deposit scheme for cans which is probably a contributory factor to the low APL for cans in Ontario. Differences in the characteristics of survey areas and the other determinants of litter will affect the absolute value of the APL's but should not affect the relative APL's.

Thus the relative APL's would only be affected by the second, third and fourth problem areas. The net effect of these counteracting forces would be small and will probably not alter the results of the APL analysis and the conclusions stated above in Section 4.c.1.

However, the beverage sales figure that was used to calculate the APL's in Tables 4.10 and 4.11 includes both 'on' premise and 'off' premise beverage consumption. Littering from 'on' premise sales would be considerably less than littering from 'off' premise sales and since returnables form a larger proportion of 'on' premise sales this factor must be taken into account.

Information was obtained on the distribution of 'off' premise beverage sales between the containers for Sweden (SWE 6) and from Metal Box for the UK data (UK 12). These figures are shown in Tables 4.12 and 4.13 and the revised APL's for 'off' premise beverage consumption are calculated for each container.

Table 4.12. THE DISTRIBUTION OF LITTERED BEER AND SOFT DRINK CONTAINERS AND 'OFF' PREMISE SALES BETWEEN THREE ALTERNATIVE CONTAINERS FOR THE UK: 1972

BEVERAGE CONTAINER	OFF PREMISE SALES IN EACH CONTAINER (MILLIONS)	No. FOUND IN LITTER SURVEY	APL ORIGINAL	APL REVISED
Bottle returnable ...	1,700	138	0.02	0.08
Non-returnable	<685	271	0.40	>0.40
Metal can	<1,405	1,185	0.84	>0.84

SOURCE: UK 4, UK 12, UK 17.

Table 4.13. THE DISTRIBUTION OF TOTAL BEVERAGE SALES, 'OFF' PREMISE BEVERAGE SALES AND BEVERAGE LITTER FOR THREE ALTERNATIVE CONTAINERS FOR SWEDEN

BEVERAGE CONTAINER	% OF TOTAL BEVERAGE SALES (1)	% OF OFF PREMISE BEVERAGE SALES (2)	% OF TOTAL LITTER (3)	APL ORIGINAL (3):(1)	APL REVISED
Bottle-returnable ...	60.5	42.3	1.2	0.02	0.05
Non-returnable	13.7	21.2	2.4	0.18	0.21
Metal can	19.7	32.0	4.3	0.22	0.22

NOTES:
1. The figures for total and 'off' premise beverage sales do not sum to 100% due to the inclusion of plastic bottles and draught beer in the Swedish data (SWE 6).
2. The % figures are a weighted version of the container mix figures for soft drinks and beer given in Section 2.
3. This data only includes beer and carbonated soft drinks. Since these beverages account for the greatest proportion of containers likely to be littered, this should not greatly affect the results.

SOURCE: SWE 5, SWE 6.

Tables 4.12 and 4.13 show that the analysis of 'off' premise sales raises the APL's for all containers, especially the returnable bottle. But a comparison of the revised APL's shows that the metal cans are still littered 4-10 times as frequently as a returnable bottle and that the non-returnable bottle is littered 4-5 times as frequently as the returnable bottle.

4.c.3. Summary

Thus it can be seen that there is increasing public concern over the problem of litter and that the beverage containers as a whole contribute significantly to this concern. Analysis of the individual beverage containers shows that the average propensity of the metal can and non-returnable bottle to be littered (APL) and to appear in accumulated litter are very much greater than the APL of the returnable bottle with respect to both total beverage sales and 'off' premise beverage sales in each container.

4.d. Pollution

Table 4.14 shows the air and water pollution caused by 5 container systems, according to an American EPA study (US 6). This shows that

Table 4.14. SUMMARY OF AIR AND WATER POLLUTION FROM 5 CONTAINER SYSTEMS PER 1,000 LITRES (UNITED STATES)

	RETURNABLE BOTTLE 19 TRIP	RETURNABLE BOTTLE 10 TRIP	RETURNABLE BOTTLE 5 TRIP	NON-RETURNABLE BOTTLE	BIMETALLIC CAN	ALUMINIUM CAN	PLASTIC BOTTLE STEEL CLOSURE
Atmospheric Emissions (kg) ..	8.5	11.3	24.0	31.3	26.7	38.8	28.8
Waterborne Wastes (kg)	3.3	4.2	8.3	6.8	4.1	7.1	8.2

SOURCE: US 6.

5 trip returnable bottles cause more water pollution than all the other containers. This pollution is principally related to the packaging (71%) and bottle filling and washing (21%) processes. However caustic Soda rather than detergents is used in the wash process and these wastes are frequently used to neutralize the acid brewery wastes (US 6). However, a portion of the 5 trip returnables systems' water pollution relates to the actual bottle and this means that, when the trippage increase to 10, the returnable bottle causes less pollution, even when the water pollution from the return and filling processes are taken into account, than all the other containers with the exception of the metal can. The 19 trip 'on' premise returnable bottle also causes considerably less water pollution, only 3.3 kgs., largely due to the reduced packaging requirements of the 3 trip paper packaging and the higher trippage rate.

The metal cans cause more air pollution than both the 5 and 10 trip returnable bottles. The major sources of the aluminium can's air pollution are the particulate emissions from the refining of bauxite ore and the fluoride and carbon-monoxide emissions from the aluminium smelting processes, which also result in considerable water pollution. The pollution resulting from energy generation is included in the figures in Table 4.14 for all the container systems and the high air pollution associated with the aluminium can is principally due to the large electricity demands of aluminium smelting. This air pollution, mostly sulphur oxides and nitrogen oxides, from electricity generation would have been a lower figure if the aluminium industry's mix of fuels for electrical energy, with its higher proportion of the clean hydro electricity, had been used rather than the national fuel mix which the EPA actually used for reasons given later in the energy section (4.f). The sulphur oxides, hydrogen sulphide, ammonia and particulate emissions from the steel strip manufacturing process and the pollution related to the aluminium top are the principal sources of the bimetallic can's air pollution.

For glass bottles 55% of the air pollution caused by the non-returnable system relates to the bottle itself, mostly in the form of hydrocarbon, sulphur oxides, nitrogen oxides and particulate emissions from the raw materials processing and the glass container manufacture. The air pollution is lowest for the 10 trip and 5 trip returnable bottle since the amortization, by trippage, of this bottle related air pollution outweighs the air pollution caused by the packaging manufacture, mostly particulates and sulphur oxides, and the return and washing process which is made up principally of carbon monoxide and nitrogen oxides emission.

The plastic ABS (Acrylonitril - polyButadiene - Styrene) bottle comes midway in the air pollution ranking causing more air pollution than the returnable bottle and bimetallic can but less than the non-returnable bottle and aluminium can. This air pollution is principally in the form of hydrocarbon, nitrogen oxides and sulphur oxides emissions. The plastic bottle causes more water pollution than all the other non-returnable containers and nearly as much as the 5 trip returnable.

The above analysis yields a pollution impact ranking which is shown in Table 4.15 where 1 refers to best and 6 refers to worst. Thus the 10 trip returnable causes the least air pollution and the aluminium can causes the largest air pollution.

Table 4.15. POLLUTION IMPACT RANKING OF 5 CONTAINER TYPES

POLLUTION	RETURNABLE BOTTLE 10 TRIP	RETURNABLE BOTTLE 5 TRIP	NON-RETURNABLE BOTTLE	CAN BI-METALLIC	CAN ALUMINIUM	PLASTIC (ABS) BOTTLE
Air pollution ..	1	2	5	3	6	4
Water pollution .	2	6	3	1	4	5

SOURCE: Table 4 (US 6).

The above pollution impact ranking only takes into account the 11 air and 13 water pollution categories considered in the EPA study (US 6). It does not take into account pollution impact in the form of aesthetic blight of the industrial solid wastes caused by the extraction of the raw materials. This is most significant for the mining of the iron ore and the refining of the alumina for the bi-metallic and aluminium cans as can be seen in Table 4.16 which shows the industrial solid waste generated by the six alternative container systems.

Table 4.16. SUMMARY OF INDUSTRIAL SOLID WASTE GENERATION BY THE ALTERNATIVE CONTAINER SYSTEM PER 1,000 GALLS - BEER/SOFT DRINKS UNITED STATES

	10 TRIP RETURNABLE BOTTLE	5 TRIP RETURNABLE BOTTLE	NON-RETURNABLE BOTTLE	STEEL CAN	ALUMINIUM CAN	PLASTIC BOTTLE STEEL CLOSURE
Industrial Solid Waste (cu. fit.)	8.91	14.94	33.46	93.00	36.13	7.21

SOURCE: US 6.

The 11 air and 13 water pollution categories were all considered equally on a weight basis by the EPA study. However this does not take into account the relative toxicity and damage costs caused by each emission category. Thus one kg of cyanide pollution is more harmful than one kg of particulate emissions and this can be seen most vividly with reference to the aluminium smelting industry which is more concerned about the fluoride emissions than the carbon monoxide emission, even though carbon monoxide constitutes a larger portion of the total weight of emissions (US 6).

Therefore, the figures in Table 4.14 do not give a true picture of the pollution damage caused by each container system, and this pollution damage can only be measured if one can ascertain some set of qualitative weights of the relative damage caused by the various pollutants. Unfortunately, it was the lack of appropriate data that prevented the EPA report from evaluating such weights. The Swiss data illustrated in Table 4.17, attempts to evaluate the damage costs of each pollutant by weighting each pollutant emission by the ratio of actual to permissible emissions. This shows that the returnable glass bottle, with a trippage of 20, incurs the least pollution damage, as here defined, followed closely by the paper carton with the metal can and the non-returnable glass and plastic bottles causing nearly twice as much pollution damage.

The Swiss study in Table 4.17 included the air pollution from the consumers' transport to and from the shopping centre on the basis of 5 km being travelled per 24 containers and this pollution, which was a significant portion of total pollution in the Swiss study, was not included in the American study; this latter study did, however, include the pollution from all the other transport requirements of the various container systems.

The Swiss study also produced a ranking for water pollution which showed that the returnable bottle (20 trips) caused the least water pollution while the metal can and paper carton caused the greatest water pollution. The difference between these results and the American results in Table 4.15 can be explained by the high trippage of 20 used in the Swiss study and differences between the two countries' methods of pollution control. There is a certain substitutability between different forms of pollution depending upon the pollution control technique. For example, emission gases can be reduced by air pollution control methods but the resulting residue can become solid waste (land pollution) or be discharged to a waterbody (water pollution). The geographic and economic characteristics of each country will determine the type of pollution control used and hence the type of pollution generated.

The German data illustrated in Table 4.18 splits up the water and air pollution into two specific categories. This shows that the returnable bottle causes the least pollution for both air and water. The bi-metallic can causes more air pollution but less water pollution than the non-returnable bottle.

The studies analysed above show considerable disagreement over the pollution ranking of the container systems. Thus the American study (US 6) shows the metal can to cause less water and air pollution than the non-returnable bottle while the German study produced reverse ranking for air pollution and the Swiss study shows the metal can to cause the most water pollution. These differences are due to different data collection and measurement methods, different pollution control methods used in each country (the emission values in each study represent emissions after current pollution control devices have been applied) and different trippage values.

The general picture that emerges is that the returnable bottle causes the least air pollution but may, at low trippages cause more water pollution than the non-returnable bottle and can; a combined water and air pollution ranking of the non-returnable containers would probably rank the non-returnable bottle and can equally and give the aluminium can and plastic bottle the least favourable ranking. However, the resolution of the different studies' results is a minor problem compared to the problem of weighting in terms of damage costs, the

Table 4.17. AIR POLLUTION FROM 5 CONTAINER SYSTEMS
(SWITZERLAND)

CONTAINER SYSTEM	EMISSIONS [1] GRAMS PER 1,000 LITRE	RANKING
Plastic Bottle (PVC)	147,000	(5)
Non-returnable Bottle	145,600	(4)
20 trip Returnable Bottle .	75,900	(1)
Metal Can	127,500	(3)
Paper Carton	76,700	(2)

NOTE:
1. Emissions include dust, carbon monoxide, chlorinated hydrocarbons, hydrocarbons, nitrogen oxides, sulphur dioxide, chlorine, hydrogen chloride, fluorine compounds and ammonia. The total emission figures are obtained by weighting each emission level by the ratio of actual emissions to permissible emission standards. This ratio is taken to be a measure of the importance of the emission level actually achieved. In formal terms:

$$\text{Total emissions} = \sum \frac{e_i}{mg_i/m^3}$$

where e_i = actual emissions of pollutant i in grams per 1,000 litres.

mg_i/m^3 = permissible level for pollutant i measured in mg per cubic metre.

SOURCE: SWI 1.

Table 4.18. POLLUTION IMPACT OF CONTAINER USE
PER 100 LITRES OF BEER - GERMANY

CONTAINER	AIR POLLUTION		WATER POLLUTION	
	Dust (g)	SO_2 (g)	BOD (g)	$CaCl_2$ (kg)
Returnable Bottle (25 trips)	2.8	25.9	31.0	0.6
Non-Returnable Bottle	57.4	535.0	250.3	11.2
Bimetallic Can	124.1	672.0	187.0	-

SOURCE: FRG 2.

different mix of water and air pollutants generated by each container system. The one study (SWI 1) that attempts to do this shows that the returnable system incurs lower pollution damage costs. This constitutes an external benefit to the returnable container system; however it is felt (SWE 4) that the pollution problem caused by the beverage container is probably better solved by a national pollution control programme since it is unlikely that beverage container pollution is a significant enough proportion of total national pollution to justify intervention in the beverage container market on this ground alone, especially when one considers the lack of information.

4.e. Hygiene and Health problems

Beverage containers create health and hygiene problems in the form of injuries from broken glass and ring pull tabs, environmental pollution from beverage container manufacture, distribution and disposal, especially in substandard landfill sites where odour and vermin problems can arise. These aspects were mentioned in Sections 4.b, 4.c and 4.d and will not be considered further here.

This section considers the health and hygiene problems related to the storage of returned bottles, the contamination of the beverage by bacteria and foreign bodies and the possible toxic effects of the beverage container on the beverage, which have been the principal cause of bans on the use of PVC for certain beverages.

The Vermont Highway Litter Evaluation Committee (US 19) cities reports of sanitation problems of odour and flies, relating to the storage of returned bottles, especially in the summer. But these reports were not verified or substantiated by the Committee. Various sources (US 36, US 37, UK 31) indicate that retailers do perceive that returnables may create sanitation problems and this is one of the reasons given by retailers for preferring and selling non-returnables instead of returnables. Although in this sense the sanitation advantages of the non-returnable will, to a certain extent, already be internalized in the current market situation. The actions of the public health inspectors will play a part in this internalization process.

There is concern over the contamination of beverages in returnable bottles by foreign substances such as vermin, dirt and mould (UK 11, US 17, US 21). However, the returnable bottles are subject to a thorough clearning by hot caustic soda and hot water sprays which sterilize the bottles and should remove almost all impurities from the bottle (US 17); any remaining impurities should be detected in the inspection stage, where a series of inspection lights or an electronic inspection device is used.

Unfortunately, there is insufficient information to substance and estimate the size of the contamination problem for returnable bottles. Based on the interviews with the industries concerned, Stern (US 17) feels that the final probability of the bottle containing a foreign substance is very low. The Ontario report (CAN 1) says that "while instances (of contamination) have occurred, they were not of sufficient concern to warrant special consideration. According to the Ministry of Health, there is not a significant enough public hazard to ban the refillable plastic jug". The report also says that all containers are equally satisfactory at protecting milk from bacteriological contamination. Stern (US 17) also shows evidence that non-returnable bottles and cans have themselves been found subject to contamination by foreign substances. Thus it would be necessary to evaluate the extra hygiene problems caused by the returnable over the non-returnable.

The fact that there has been a reduction in recent years in the number of complaints about foreign substances may be due more to stricter enforcement of food regulations and hygiene standards and improvements in cleaning processes than the shift from returnables to non-returnables. The hygiene problem of beverage containers should be more efficiently approached by stronger regulation of public hygiene and product quality standards, which would then leave it to the individual bottler and retailer to evaluate his own relative probabilities for the sanitation and contamination problems likely to be caused by each type of container and decide whether to improve the cleaning and storage process or switch to non-returnables.

4.f. Energy and materials use

The energy requirements of the current beverage container system are estimated for the United States to be 0.50% of total US energy consumption (US 2), and for Sweden to be 0.35% of total Swedish energy consumption (SWE 4).

Energy will be required at various stages of the beverage container system (as highlighted for glass bottles in the Flow Chart in Fig. 4.1) and can be split up into five principal components. The energy required: (1) to process and extract the raw materials from which the containers are made; (2) to manufacture the container; (3) to manufacture supplementary products such as closures and packaging; (4) to fill and transport the containers to the retailers; and (5) to finally dispose of the container or, in the case of returnables, to return empty containers for cleaning, filling and re-use.

These energy requirements will differ for all the alternative beverage containers on account of the different distribution methods inherent in the container system (i.e. whether it is a returnable or a one way system) and on account of the different characteristics of the materials used. Thus glass is heavier and more susceptible to breakages than the other materials and hence will entail greater energy for the transportation and packaging; while another container material (e.g. aluminium) may entail a very energy intensive process for raw material processing and hence, the energy requirements related to the beverage container manufacture will be very large. This shows that,

Figure 4.1

MATERIALS FLOW FOR GLASS CONTAINER SYSTEMS

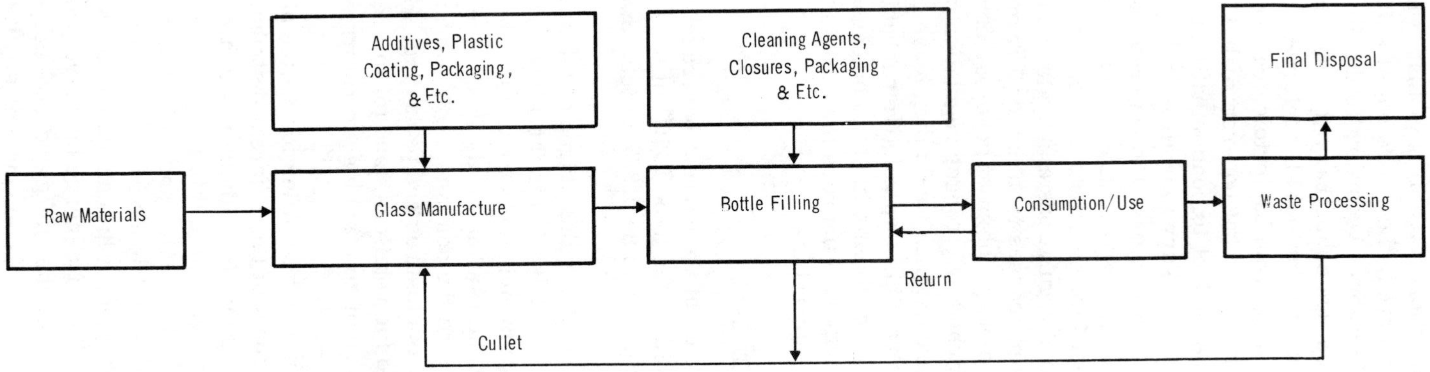

Source : US 6

in comparing the beverage containers, it is necessary to compare the total system energy requirements for each beverage container system (from the processing of the raw materials to the disposal of wastes) and not just one part of the system.

There has been considerable growth over the last few years in systems energy analysis, which enables an evaluation of the energy requirements of the various container systems.

4.f.1. Energy Comparison of Various Alternative Beverage Container Systems for Soft Drinks and Beer

The following tables (4.19-4.21), based on a RTI study (US 2), show the energy required by the various process stages for each alternative beverage container system in Therms* per 100 litres of beer or soft drinks delivered to the consumer. The percentage distribution is included as well in order to show which is the process stage that requires the most significant portion of the total energy requirements.

Table 4.19. THE ENERGY REQUIREMENTS BY PROCESS STAGE OF A 12 oz (34 cl) BI-METALLIC CAN SYSTEM FOR BEER (1974)

PROCESS STAGE	THERMS PER 100 LITRES	%
Can manufacture a)	10.82	88.5
Packaging	0.84	6.9
Filling + Distribution	0.54	4.5
Waste disposal	0.014	0.1
Total	12.21	100

a) This includes the energy to extract and process the raw materials as well as the energy to manufacture the containers.

SOURCE: US 2.

It is evident from Tables 4.19-4.21 that, for the non-returnable one way beverage container systems (especially the all aluminium can), the energy related to the beverage container accounts for a very large proportion of the total energy requirements - 87% for the bimetallic can, 92% for the aluminium can and 68% for the glass bottle system. However, a similar picture does not emerge for the returnable glass

* Throughout this Section the Therms has been used as the energy unit - 1 Therm = 10^5 BTU = 25,200 Kcal = 105,500 Kj.

Table 4.20. THE ENERGY REQUIREMENTS,
BY PROCESS STAGE, OF A 12 oz (34 cl) ALUMINIUM CAN
SYSTEM FOR BEER (1974)

PROCESS STAGE	THERMS PER 100 LITRES	%
Can manufacture [a]	17.3	92.5
Packaging	0.84	4.5
Filling + Distribution	0.54	2.9
Waste disposal	0.012	0.1
Total	18.7	100

a) See note (a) Table 4.19.
SOURCE: US 2.

Table 4.21. THE ENERGY REQUIREMENTS,
BY PROCESS STAGE, OF A NON-RETURNABLE 12 oz (34 cl)
GLASS BOTTLE SYSTEM FOR BEER (1975)

PROCESS STAGE	THERMS PER 100 LITRES	%
Bottle [a]	7.6	66.7
Closure and label	0.52	4.7
Packaging	2.09	18.3
Filling + Distribution	1.02	9.0
Waste disposal	0.21	1.2
Total	11.4	100

a) See note (a) Table 4.19.
SOURCE: US 2.

bottle system since, under the returnable system, a glass bottle will be returned for refilling and re-use a number of times. The energy requirements for the returnable system can therefore be usefully split into those elements that are independent of trippage, which are those stages in the process of delivering beverages that consume the same amount of energy, regardless of whether a new or a returned bottle is used, and the trippage dependent elements. These are the process stages of the returnable system for which the energy requirements will vary directly with the trippage achieved.

Table 4.22. TRIPPAGE INDEPENDENT ENERGY REQUIREMENTS OF A 12 oz (34 cl) RETURNABLE GLASS BOTTLE SYSTEM FOR BEER (1975)

PROCESS STAGE	THERMS PER 100 LITRES
Closure and label	0.53
Packaging	1.61
Filling and Distribution	2.22
Waste Disposal	0.002
Total	4.36

SOURCE: US 2.

Table 4.23 shows the energy required for the manufacture and disposal of each returnable bottle. This is greater than the energy related to the non-returnable glass bottle (compare 13.19 with 7.6 in Table 4.21) on account of the greater weight and durability characteristics of the returnable bottle. However, these trippage dependent energy requirements will be amortized over the life and number of trips of a returnable bottle. Thus, Table 4.24 shows the total energy requirements for a 10 trip returnable system.

Table 4.23. TRIPPAGE DEPENDENT ENERGY REQUIREMENTS FOR A 12 oz (34 cl) RETURNABLE GLASS BOTTLE SYSTEM WITH A TRIPPAGE OF ONE - BEER (1975)

PROCESS STAGE	THERMS PER 100 LITRES
Bottle	13.19
Waste disposal (glass)	0.17
Total	13.36

SOURCE: US 2.

Table 4.24. shows that the energy related to the packaging and distribution processes form a much larger proportion of total energy requirements and the energy related to the bottle forms a lower percentage under a returnable system than under a non-returnable system. These percentages, of course, depend upon the trippage figure used.

Table 4.24. ENERGY REQUIREMENTS FOR A 12 oz (34 cl) RETURNABLE BOTTLE SYSTEM WITH A TRIPPAGE OF 10 - BEER (1975)

PROCESS STAGE	THERMS PER 100 LITRES	%	
Trippage Dependent factors:			
- Bottle	1.3	22.9	23.3
- Waste disposal (glass) ..	0.02	0.4	
Trippage Independent factors:			
- Closure + Label	0.53	9.3	
- Packaging	1.61	28.4	76.7
- Filling + Distribution ..	2.22	39.0	
- Waste disposal	0.002	-	
Total	5.68	100	

SOURCE: US 2.

The breakdown between trippage dependent and trippage independent requirements is useful in that it enables the calculation of the trippage (T*) that the returnable system must attain in order to break even in energy terms with the non-returnable systems:

$$\frac{E_{Dep}}{T^*} + E_{Indep} \leq E_{nrb}$$

This can be seen in the above equation where E_{nrb} is the total energy requirements of the non-returnable system, E_{Indep} is the returnable systems energy requirements that are independent of trippage and E_{Dep} the trippage dependent energy requirements of a returnable system. T* is the breakeven trippage which amortizes the trippage dependent requirements so that the total energy requirements are less for a returnable system than for a non-returnable system.

The values for E_{nrb}, E_{Indep} and E_{Dep} can be obtained from Tables 4.19-4.23 to produce the breakeven trippages for a returnable system, as shown in Table 4.25.

The soft drinks beverage situation will differ from the beer situation on account of the fact that the soft drink bottle has to be 22% (US 2) heavier than its beer counterpart, in order to withstand the higher internal pressure of soft drinks carbonation. Thus extra energy will be required to manufacture and distribute the heavier bottle and also in the filling process. However, in the United States the soft drinks industry is less centralized and, along with the greater space utilization properties of soft drinks containers, this means that in fact the transportation energy requirements are lower for soft drinks in the USA.

Table 4.25. BREAKEVEN TRIPPAGES (T*) FOR THE 12 oz (34 cl) RETURNABLE GLASS BOTTLE SYSTEM IN COMPARISON WITH 3 ALTERNATIVE NON-RETURNABLE CONTAINER SYSTEMS FOR BEER

ALTERNATIVE NON-RETURNABLE SYSTEM	BREAKEVEN TRIPPAGE T*
Aluminium can	0.93
Bimetallic can	1.71
Non-Returnable glass bottle	1.91

NOTE: The figure of less than one for the aluminium can arises because the total energy requirements for the aluminium can are greater than the combined trippage dependent and independent energy requirements for returnable bottles.
SOURCE: Adapted from RTI (US 2) data in Tables 4.19-4.23.

The total energy requirements for the alternative beverage container systems for soft drinks are given in Table 4.26, which also includes data for 2 types of plastic non-returnable bottles: A polyester (PET) and an Acrylonitrile/Styrene (AN/S) bottle. These plastic bottle use less energy than the other non-returnable containers but still considerably more than a 10 trip returnable.

The bimetallic and aluminium cans are the same weight for both beer and soft drinks and the extra energy required for soft drink filling is offset by the reduced distribution energy, so that the total energy requirements for the two can systems are virtually unchanged. The heavier soft drink bottle raises the total energy requirements of the non-returnable glass bottle system and the trippage dependent energy requirements for the returnable bottle. Although the lower transportation and packaging requirements of soft drinks mean that the trippage independent energy requirements are reduced so that the net effect is for the total energy requirements of a 10 trip returnable glass bottle to be less for soft drinks than they are for beer.

This rise in the trippage dependent energy requirements for the returnable soft drink bottle means that the breakeven trippage rates will be greater for soft drinks than they were for beer, as can be seen in Table 4.27.

Table 4.26. TOTAL ENERGY REQUIREMENTS, IN THERMS PER 100 LITRES, OF BEVERAGE CONTAINER SYSTEMS FOR SOFT DRINKS

CONTAINER SYSTEM	THERMS PER 100 LITRES
12 oz aluminium can	18.7
12 oz bimetallic can	12.3
Non-returnable bottle:	
- 16 oz glass	12.02
- 16 oz plastic (PET) [1]	11.54
- 16 oz plastic (AN/S)	11.57
16 oz returnable glass bottle:	
- trippage dependent factors	18.2
- trippage independent factors ..	1.8
Total for a returnable glass bottle system with a trippage of 10	3.6

1. PET = Polyester
   AN/S = Acrylonitrile/Styrene
SOURCE: US 2.

Table 4.27. BREAKEVEN TRIPPAGE RATES REQUIRED SO THAT A 16 oz (45 cl) RETURNABLE BOTTLE SYSTEM REQUIRES THE SAME ENERGY INPUTS AS ALTERNATIVE CONTAINER SYSTEMS FOR SOFT DRINKS

ALTERNATIVE SYSTEM	BREAKEVEN TRIPPAGE RATE
Bimetallic can	1.86
Aluminium can	1.06
Non-returnable bottle:	
- glass	1.78
- plastic (PET)	1.94
- plastic (AN/S)	1.93

SOURCE: US 2.

4.f.2. Critical Appraisal of the RTI data

The previous tables 4.19-4.27 were all based on data in the RTI study - Energy and Economic Impacts of Mandatory Deposits (US 2). This data source was used because it is a very thorough and recent study which conveniently breaks down the energy requirements by process stages and into trippage dependent and independent requirements. This enables one to make the useful calculations of the minimum number of trips that a returnable bottle system must attain before it requires less energy inputs than the principal alternative container systems.

However, it has been brought to our attention (UK 11, UK 12) that the RTI data is subject to criticisms and, being based on American data, may not be relevant to the situation in Europe. Results were therefore obtained from other European and American studies (see Table 4.28) so as to get an overall picture of the energy comparisons and an attempt is made to explain the differences between the studies' results and show whether, and if so in what direction, the RTI results should be modified to allow for the different structural situations in Europe and America.

It is beyond the scope of this study to evaluate the technical engineering relations that underlie the data in the RTI study (e.g. the energy efficiency of the manufacturing and raw material processing stages etc.). However, the six major assumptions that underlie the RTI results were analysed to show whether the assumptions used by RTI differ significantly from the situations experienced in other European and American studies.

(1). It was stated earlier that it is necessary to analyse the energy requirements of the <u>total</u> beverage container <u>system</u>. This has been done in the RTI study and most of the other studies (EPA US 6, HANNON US 8, SWE 5, SWE 3) but was not done for UK 8 (Incpen) which only considers the energy requirements related to the beverage container.

(2). Trippage. The energy savings for the returnable bottle system depend on the trippage figure that is used. The RTI data gets round this problem by calculating trippage dependent and independent energy requirements so that the current 'on' premise and 'off' premise trippage rates for each country (estimates of which were given in Section 3.c) can be inserted to show the resulting energy consumptions.

(3). Container Size. It has been shown (CAN 1, US 17, US 2 and UK 7) that the energy requirements to deliver a certain volume of beverage (say 100 litres) will be less for a large container than a small container. Therefore it is necessary that the comparison of alternative container systems is consistent with respect to volume. RTI achieves this for beer but not for soft drinks where 16 oz. glass and plastic bottles are compared with the 12 oz. aluminium and bimetallic cans. This means that the breakeven trippage figures for the returnable bottle, against the two types of cans, should be adjusted upwards but not by a great deal.

Table 4.19, 4.20, 4.21 and 4.24 show that the energy requirements related to the container, the packaging and the distribution form a large portion of the total energy requirements for the alternative systems and therefore changes in the assumptions concerning these three factors will have a significant impact on the energy comparison.

(4). Energy related to the container. The RTI data in Tables 4.19 - 4.26 relate to the current position and only consider current conventional beer and soft drinks containers. No allowance is made here for future reductions in the beverage containers energy requirements that US 16 forecasts to result from the development of new products (e.g. the all steel can), and improvements in process efficiencies and reductions in container weights. This issue is considered in more details in Section 5.k where we analyse the effects of technological change on the beverage container situation. These energy savings, as US 16 stresses, will occur through the normal operation of market forces, in the absence of beverage container legislation. The reason for this is that energy has a current market price, increases in which will lead to economies in its use. However it must be remembered that an external cost analysis should ignore this internal cost element and only consider the external costs of energy use. Therefore if one considers that energy is an issue that warrants special consideration (i.e. the social valuation of energy exceeds the current markets price) then one should also consider that further energy saving in one form or another in excess of these markets induced conservation, are required.

The RTI study assumes a zero recycling rate for post consumer containers but US 16 showed that considerable energy savings could be achieved by recycling cans, especially aluminium cans, so that this aspect is considered in detail in section 5.j. This showed that the recycling rates were fairly low in most countries and not sufficient to alter the energy rankings of the alternatives containers shown in the RTI study.

It has also been noted (NETH 10) that RTI data overstates the disadvantageous position of the bimetallic can since a 3 piece metal can is used in America while in Europe a lighter 2 piece (DWI process) can is currently used.

Also the energy requirements for the aluminium can depend upon the manner in which the electricity used by aluminium manufacturers is treated. RTI distributes this electricity between energy sources (coal, oil, gas, hydro electric) in relation to the aluminium industry's actual use of a high proportion of hydrogenerated electricity. Other studies (US 6) use the national mix of energy sources for electricity generation on the grounds that the aluminium industry's use of a cheap and efficient source means that other users of electricity (now using the fossil fuel mix) are prevented from using the cheap hydro source and this national mix will be particularly relevant where a national grid for electricity is apparent. RTI estimates (US 2) that the different methods of treating electricity results in a 10% difference in total energy requirements for the aluminium can systems.

(5). Packaging. Packaging forms a significant portion of the total energy requirements for the glass bottle system, especially the returnable system. Various European sources (NETH 7, DK 1) suggest that American railroad bye laws result in more supplementary packaging being used in America than Europe, where returnable plastic crates with a very high trippage, are frequently used. Therefore the energy requirements for the supplementary packaging used in beverage distribution in Europe would probably be lower than the figures given in the RTI study.

(6). Distribution. The beverage market for the United States can be expected to be more dispersed than its European counterpart, on account of the greater population density in Europe. Therefore the distribution energy requirements will be greater for the US in the RTI study than for a European beverage container study. Table 4.24 and 4.19 to 4.21 show that the distribution energy requirements for the returnable bottle are much greater than for either the non-returnable bottle or the can; in the light of this factor, the European returnable bottle's relative position would be improved.

Table 4.28 shows the results of many European and American studies into the energy requirements of beverage containers. It has been noted (UK 28) that there is some divergence between the actual results generated by these separate studies. This will be due in part to the different situations apparent in the individual countries and the different values that the separate studies place on the assumptions (1)-(6) above.

Table 4.29 gives a tabular representation of these different assumptions and shows considerable gaps in the data on the studies' assumptions, especially for the European countries: this was one of the principal reasons for our concentration on American data. Each country will need to fill in the values for the assumptions that are relevant to them in order to get some impression of their own individual position in the energy comparisons.

Although there is some discrepancy between the absolute values given by the various studies, the relative ranking is fairly uniform throughout all the studies with the returnable system requiring the least energy requirements for soft drinks, even at very low trippages of 3, followed by the bimetallic can and the non-returnable bottle with the aluminium can requiring significantly the largest energy requirements in all the studies. The position is very similar for beer.

Unfortunately, good data is not as readily available for the other beverages (milk, mineral water, wine and spirits). The data we were able to obtain is summarized in Table 4.30. Although there is a discrepancy between the absolute values for some of the data, the relative positions accord with the ranking for the carbonated beverages and also show the potential energy savings of a refillable plastic system over the refillable glass bottle and non-refillable plastic and glass bottle systems. The favourable position of light and flimsy non-refillables (e.g. the paper carton and plastic pouch) is also evident.

Table 4.28. ENERGY REQUIRED TO PROVIDE FILLABLE MATERIAL FOR 100 LITRES OF BEER AND SOFT DRINKS IN EACH CONTAINER SYSTEM THERMS PER 100 LITRES

COUNTRY STUDY	BEVERAGE	ALUMINIUM CAN	BIMETALLIC CAN	NON-RETURNABLE BOTTLE GLASS	NON-RETURNABLE BOTTLE PLASTIC	RETURNABLE GLASS BOTTLE	RETURNABLE GLASS (TRIPPAGE)	SOURCE
UK	All Carbonated Beverages	9.6	6.7	7.1		5.4	(3)	UK 8
USA								
1. RTI	Soft Drinks	18.7	12.3	11.4	11.5	3.6	(10)	US 2
	Beer	18.7	12.2	17.3		5.1	(10)	(see note 1)
2. Hannon	Soft Drinks	21.2	15.4			7.2	(8)	US 8
						6.4	(15)	
3. EPA	Beer	n/a	15.4	15.8		5.2	(19)	US 6 (see note 2)
	Beer	19.8	14.2	17.0		11.3	(5*)	(see note 1)
						7.5	(5)	
						5.7	(10)	
						4.2	(19)	
Canada	Soft Drinks	n/a	14.8	20.1		9.1	(10)	CAN 1
	Beer	n/a	14.0	n/a		5.7	(21.5)	
Sweden	Beer	n/a	8.3	11.3	5.8	4.2	(8)	SWE 3 (see note 4)
						3.2	(19)	
	All Beverages	n/a	8.2	11.2		3.2	(19)	SWE 5
	Wines and Spirits					9.2	(2)	
Germany	Soft Drinks	12.4	9.5	10.1	9.5	7.7	(3)	FRG 3
						4.2	(8)	(see note 3)
							(19)	
Switzerland	n/a	n/a	10.0*	8.0		1.2	(20)	SWI 1*, SWI 4
Netherlands	All Carbonated Beverages	n/a	n/a	8.0	4.0	1.7	(10)	NETH 10

NOTE 1. The 5 trip returnable bottle system in the EPA study (US 6) uses a 3 trip returnable six pack carrier as in the RTI study (US 2).
NOTE 2. However the EPA study also considered a one trip returnable six pack carrier and this is evaluated in the 5* trip returnable bottle system.
NOTE 3. The plastic bottle in the German study (FRG 3) relates to a light plastic bottle. A heavy plastic bottle would require 12.8 therms per 100 litres.
NOTE 4. The plastic bottle in the Swedish study (SWE 3) is a Rigello Bottle.

76

Table 4.29. A SUMMARY OF THE IMPORTANT ASSUMPTIONS MADE IN THE ENERGY STUDIES SHOWN IN TABLE 4.28

ASSUMPTION	RTI (US 2) BEER	RTI (US 2) SOFT DRINKS	EPA (US 6) BEER	HANNON (US 8) BEER	HANNON (US 8) SOFT DRINKS	INCPEN (UK 8)	CANADA (CAN 1)	SWEDEN (SWE 3)
1. Date of study	1975	1975	1974	1973	1973	n/a	1972	1973
2. Total system approach	Yes	Yes	Yes	Yes	Yes	No	Yes	Yes
3. Container size	Equal	Different (see note 2)	Equal	Equal	Different (see note 2)	Different (see note 3)	Equal	Different (see note 3)
4. Recycling % rate for post consumer aliminium cans	0%	0%	15%	0%	0%	n/a	20% (see note 4)	n/a
5. Treatment of Fuel source mix for the generation of electricity used in aluminium smelting	Actual Industry Mix	Actual Industry Mix	National mix	n/a	n/a	n/a	n/a	n/a
6. Transportation distances								
a) container brewery	n/a	n/a	n/a	300-345 miles		n/a	n/a	n/a
b) brewery retailer	235-425 miles	150 miles	n/a	231 miles		n/a	n/a	n/a

NOTES:
1. The Incpen study only considers the energy to produce and deliver the beverage containers and closures. It does not include the energy used in the filling and distribution processes of beverage production.
2. The glass bottle (usually 16 oz.) is larger than the metal containers (usually 12 oz.). This requires one to adjust upwards the figures for returnable and non-returnable glass bottle system's figures.
3. In these cases the glass bottles are smaller and therefore their figures should be adjusted downwards. In the Swedish case (SWE 3) only the returnable glass bottle is smaller.
4. The recycling figure for Canada (CAN 1) relates to the recycling of bimetallic not aluminium cans.

Table 4.30. ENERGY REQUIREMENTS OF NON-CARBONATED BEVERAGES FILLABLE MATERIAL THERMS PER 100 LITRES

BEVERAGE	COUNTRY	PAPER CARTON NON-REFILLABLE	POUCH	PLASTIC NON-REFILLABLE BOTTLE	PLASTIC REFILLABLE BOTTLE	(TRIPPAGE)	GLASS BOTTLE NON-REFILLABLE	GLASS BOTTLE REFILLABLE	(TRIPPAGE)	SOURCE
1. Milk	UK	n/a	n/a	2.4	n/a	(n/a)	n/a	0.58	(25)	UK 13
	Canada	0.56-.64	.17	1.1	0.06	(200)	n/a	0.62	(n/a)	CAN 1 (note 1)
2. Wines and spirits	Canada	–	–	n/a	n/a	(n/a)	19	n/a	(n/a)	CAN 1
	Sweden	–	–	n/a	n/a	(n/a)	n/a	9.2	(2)	SWE 5
	France	–	–	3.4	–	–	9.6	2.7	(12)	–
	Netherlands	1.67	–	–	–	–	7.1	–	–	NETH 7 (note 2)
3. Mineral Water	France	–	–	2.9	n/a	(n/a)	n/a	1.5	(24)	FR 2

Notes: 1. The Canadian figures for milk relate only to the container manufacture and filling. They do not include the energy for the distribution to and from retail outlets or for the solid waste collection.
2. The Dutch wine carton refers to a paper aluminium polyethylene laminated pack weighting 50.6 grs.

Table 4.31. TRIPPAGE (T*) REQUIRED FOR A RETURNABLE GLASS BOTTLE SYSTEM TO BREAKEVEN IN THE ENERGY COMPARISON WITH ALTERNATIVE CONTAINERS SYSTEM

1. SOFT DRINK AND BEER

| STUDY SOURCE | ALTERNATIVE CONTAINER ||||
| | CAN || BOTTLE ||
	ALUMINIUM	BIMETALLIC	NON-RETURNABLE GLASS	PLASTIC
Germany (FRG 3)	1-2	3	2	1.5-2.6
RTI (US 2)	1	1.7-1.9	1.8	n/a
EPA (US 6)	1-2	3	2	n/a
Hannon (US 8)	1.2	1.5	1.5	n/a
Canada (CAN 1)	n/a	1.8-3.7	1.8-2.3	n/a
Sweden (SWE 4)	n/a	2	n/a	5-7
Metal Box (UK 11)			2-3	

2. MILK

| STUDY SOURCE | ALTERNATIVE CONTAINER |||
	PAPER	PLASTIC (PE) BOTTLE	PLASTIC POUCH
Incpen (UK 8)	3-5	3-5	7-10
Boustead (UK 13)	n/a	10	n/a

79

Thus it can be seen that a returnable system will yield considerable energy savings over the aluminium and bimetallic cans and non-returnable glass and plastic bottle systems, as long as its trippage exceeds the breakeven trippage T*.

Table 4.31 shows these breakeven trippage rates for the returnable glass bottle with respect to the seven alternative container systems. Section 3.c gives current estimates of trippage of 5-70 for soft drinks and beer and 26-200 for milk (see Table 3.4). However, these figures related to total trippages which will be a weighted average of 'on' premise and 'off' premise trippages. The 'off' premise trippage is difficult to single out and determine, but estimates for soft drinks and beer are 3 (Metal Box figure in UK 17), 7 (SWE 3) and 10 (US 6).

4.f.3. Energy inputs by fuel type

Table 4.32 shows the energy requirements for each beer container system in the USA subdivided into the three principal sources of energy. Natural gas accounts for a large proportion of the energy required to manufacture bottles and this results in the glass container systems, especially the non-returnables, requiring large inputs of hydrocarbon energy (natural gas and petroleum), so that the 5 trip returnable bottle system in fact uses more hydrocarbon energy than the bimetallic can. However, the bimetallic can uses greater inputs of coal energy.

Table 4.32. ENERGY REQUIREMENTS BY FUEL TYPE IN USA (BEER)
(THERMS PER 100 LITRES)

	RETURNABLE GLASS BOTTLE 10 TRIP	RETURNABLE GLASS BOTTLE 5 TRIP	NON-RETURNABLE GLASS	STEEL CAN	ALUMINIUM CAN
Petroleum	1.7	3.1	3.6	2.7	4.6
Natural Gas	2.3	4.2	8.6	4.6	8.2
Coal	0.9	1.8	2.8	6.3	5.8
Wood Fibre	0.7	2.1	1.7	0.04	0.04
Miscellaneous	0.08	0.15	0.26	0.6	1.2
Total	5.7	11.3	17.0	14.2	19.8

SOURCE: US 6.

Therefore, except for the case of the 10 trip returnable bottle system where the low total energy requirements mean that it entails the lowest inputs for all energy sources, it is necessary to find some weights to trade off the different rankings generated when considering different energy sources.

The choice of these weights will be eased if it is recollected that external costs and benefits are the basis for a social evaluation of beverage containers and that external costs are defined as the costs that will not be taken into account by the manufacturers. The major energy sources (coal, oil and petroleum) all have market prices and therefore the lower energy requirements of the returnables system will be reflected in lower energy costs. As Pearce and Webb (UK 20) point out, energy analysis is only relevant if there is any divergence between the market value of energy (price) and the value that society (present and future) puts on energy or the long run social opportunity cost of energy, and this difference for coal, natural gas and petroleum should be the weights used to evaluate and energy ranking of the alternative beverage containers. However, the estimation of the social opportunity cost of energy is difficult and subjective and we shall just point out the determinants of the social opportunity cost and refrain from giving a value judgement as to its relative order of magnitude.

The Ontario study (CAN 1) shows a survey result that many people are concerned about resources (raw material and energy). This concern will be determined by three factors. First is the concern that the world is using up finite sources of energy too fast and the effect that this will have on future generations, future prices and the social fabric if technology is not able to develop, in time, alternative energy sources and new reserves. Current debate continues between the optimists (e.g. Beckerman UK 14) and the pessimists (e.g. Meadows UK 15) and rests upon their respective value judgements over the belief in society's ability to overcome the problems of resource depletion through market induced conservation and technological advance. Second, there is concern about the pollution externalities of energy extraction and processing (e.g. coal trips, amenity loss in scenic areas, etc.). However, care must be taken in the analysis to ensure that this pollution is not double counted by its inclusion in both the energy and the pollution sections. Third, balance of payment considerations will induce governments to favour energy conservation in order to save imports. These three factors will result in the social opportunity cost of energy source being above their market prices and the existence of government measures to encourage energy conservation has been taken by some (US 5) to indicate that the social opportunity cost of energy is greater than its market price.

However, the analysis is complicated by the very evident existence of monopoly in the energy market, especially for petroleum, which reduces output and has raised the price of oil considerably. This has caused Kay and Mirrlees (UK 16) to suggest that the current market price for energy is above the long run social opportunity cost and that, therefore, the world is in fact, using up energy resources too slowly. A further complication is that the third factor causing concern over energy use (balance of payments) will in part be determined by the monopoly rise in international oil prices.

4.f.4. Summary of energy use

Thus it can be seen that the systems energy analysis of the current beverage containers results in a ranking where returnable glass and plastic bottles require the least energy, followed by the non-returnable plastic bottle, and the bimetallic can requiring the greatest energy. The energy savings of the returnable depends upon the returnable bottle achieving an 'on' and 'off' premise trippage of between 1 to 4 for soft drinks and beer, and 3 to 10 for milk, which are estimated to be currently attained and attainable. These energy savings should be valued in the analysis as the difference between the social opportunity cost and the market price of energy. As discussed earlier no comment is made on how much the social opportunity cost is above or below the current monopolistically determined price. The strength of the feelings expressed on the energy issue and the implementation of energy conservation programmes by many countries suggest that the social opportunity cost of energy is greater than its current market price and that therefore the energy savings of the returnable system should be considered external benefits. Even though the energy savings from using returnables in the place of non-returnables would be a very small proportion of total national energy consumption, it is felt by some (e.g. UK 27, UK 28) that these energy savings merit elaboration on account of doubts over the effectiveness of general steering measures such as energy taxes, to achieve across the board reductions in national energy consumption, and require that a piece-meal approach to energy conservation be undertaken.

4.f.5. Materials use

Conceptually any consideration of the social costs of material use may be dealt with in the same way that energy use has been treated, since both these factors come under the more general heading of natural resource use. The external cost element generally associated with natural resource use is termed 'user cost' and may be defined as the cost (loss of benefits) incurred upon third parties (future generations) by the production and consumption activities of the current generation.

The reason that these costs are not reflected in private or market price is due primarily to the time planning horizon over which decisions are made (i.e. the time horizon of a society is generally considered to be greater than that of an individual). It is therefore likely that the use of natural resources over time will occur too quickly.

Any study of the costs of materials use must therefore consider the difference between market price and social cost if the extent of this overconsumption is to be quantified. Unfortunately, no studies relevant to the beverage container issue have dealt with this aspect in the terms defined above and this must be left open for further investigation.

PART II

V

POLICY MEASURES

5.a. <u>General Criteria for Policy Selection</u>

A review of the various OECD countries' current beverage container policy proposals and enacted legislation shows that there are ten principal policy options open to governments. They are listed below:

1. Do nothing.
2. Ban non-returnable bottles and cans.
3. Require mandatory deposits be levied on all containers.
4. Oregon Bottle Bill type legislation which combines the levying of a refundable deposit with a ban on cans with detachable ring pulls.
5. A high tax on beverage containers as implemented in Norway.
6. A product charge on all packaging.
7. A low litter tax with the revenue used to finance anti-litter campaigns, as in Washington.
8. Measures to encourage standardization.
9. Encourage recycling and resource recovery.
10. Encourage research and development into product innovation.

as well as various combinations of the measures 1-10 above.

It is necessary to have some method of evaluating the costs and benefits of each of these policy options. One possible method is to see what happened in the various countries that have introduced beverage container legislation. This is considered in Sections 5.c-g below. However, there are two problems associated with this approach. First, the comparison of pre and post legislation situations will not pick up the impact solely due to the legislation. What is really required is a comparison of the post policy 'on' situation with the post policy 'off' situation that would have occured if there had been no policy. Second, the legislation studies are based mainly on American experiences and as the European delegates have rightly pointed out (UK 22, UK 12, NETH 6), this may not be relevant to the European beverage container situation. We have attempt to solve this problem by formulating a general framework which will identify the costs and benefits that could be expected to result from each policy option and will attempt to identify the critical variables that determine the size of these costs and benefits. The idea of this general framework for policy evaluation is that each country can insert the values for its own unique beverage container situation and will focus attention on the critical variable so as to maximize the benefits and minimize the costs and hence select a policy measure which produces the greatest social gain. This general framework has been subdivided between environmental benefits, economic impact costs, and impacts on the government sector.

5.a.1. Environmental Benefits

The environmental benefits of the policy measure will be any savings in the external costs that were analysed in Section 4:
 1. Solid waste generation.
 2. Litter.
 3. Pollution.
 4. Hygiene and health.
 5. Energy consumption.

The level of these environmental benefits will depend upon the size of the external costs and benefits generated by all the beverage container systems under each policy option. If the policy option should result in greater external costs than the current situation then this constitutes a cost of the policy option.

The general picture that emerges from Section 4 is that the non-returnable containers impose greater external costs than the returnable bottle and that the non-returnable bottle generates more solid waste but less litter than the metal cans. Therefore savings in these external costs can be achieved by changes in market shares in favour of returnables. The container market shares are principally determined by the costs of the alternative beverage container systems, the availability of beverages in both returnable and non-returnable containers, the consumers' value of the convenience of non-returnable containers and his perceived price differential of beverages in the alternative containers, which may differ from the net price differential if the consumer fails to 'perceive' the deposit in the gross price, or experiences difficulty in returning the bottle for refund.

However, these environmental benefits of the returnable system depend crucially upon whether the trippage achieved exceeds the break-even trippage and if so by how much. Appendix 1 shows the methodology which countries can use to derive their own estimates of 'on' and 'off' premise trippage values. The wide discrepancy between the different countries and different beverages trippage values, shown in Table 3.4, suggests a potentially fruitful avenue for research into the determinants of trippage. From the information available to us the principal determinants of 'off' premise trippage seem to be the level of the deposit and the consumer's ease of returning the bottle, which is influenced by the number of retailers/bottlers that accept returnables. There are other determinants of trippage such as the mode of distribution (e.g. the UK milkman) the durability of the bottle and the type of packaging used (e.g. the Canadian returnable 6 pack carrier) but these were felt to be either not as significant or not susceptible to policy changes. The level of the deposit must be sufficient to induce the consumer to return the bottle but a Canadian survey found that more than 70% of respondents would not be willing to pay as much as 3 ¢ for the convenience of not returning the container (CAN 1). Peaker (US 4) shows that the ease of return is a more important determinant of trippage than the level of the deposit, and that the level of the deposit must be set to ensure that the deposit plus the retailers' and bottlers' handling and transportation costs of returnables are less than the costs of purchasing a new bottle. If this is so then the retailers and bottlers will encourage returns; this is an essential condition for the achievement of higher trippage values and therefore these four variables (level of deposit, ease of return, mode of distribution, type of packaging) are the critical determinants of trippage.

The change in the container market shares will have two conflicting effects on trippage. A rise in the returnables' market share may result in lower trippages since survey results (CAN 1) show that the return rate of new purchasers will be less than the return rate of the old purchasers so that the aggregate return rate and trippage may decline. However, the rise in returnables' market share will increase the number of retailers that accept returnables and this factor will cause an increase in trippage. The net effect of these two counteracting forces is difficult to determine and will probably vary for each member state.

Two further aspects of a policy's environmental impact need to be mentioned. The first concerns the policy's impact on the level of recycling. It is necessary to determine the net effect of the direct impact of specific measures included in the policy (e.g. mandatory deposits on cans, provision encouraging the use of recycling materials, etc.) and the indirect general impact of the policy on solid waste. This indirect effect will be the result of the policy's impact on the level of solid waste and in particular the recyclable content (paper, metal, and glass), which may adversely affect the viability of one form of solid waste management - recycling and resource recovery. Correspondence with experts in this field suggests that the viability of resource recovery systems is determined principally by their capital costs and the costs of alternative disposal methods. This is especially true for the currently popular energy recovery systems for which the two factors above and the combustible components of solid waste are very much more important than its glass and metal content. Thus it is thought that the policy would not affect the decision to install a resource recovery system except in the very marginal economic circumstances.

Second, US 16 notes that a shift from non-returnables to returnables would require an initial increase in the production of returnable bottles so that the 'float' can be built up. This means that, in fact, energy consumption may increase in the first years following the policy. However depending upon the trippage achieved, the returnable system would thereafter generate annual savings in energy consumption.

According to this study (US 16) the breakeven point will occur after the second year if a trippage of 10 is achieved; if, however, a trippage of only 5 is achieved the breakeven point may not occur until after the eighth year. Thus it is necessary to undertake an investment type analysis and discount the annual energy savings in perpetuity against the initial increase in energy consumption. This requires determination of the relative social value of energy consumption now and energy consumption in the future, which will depend, in part, on the question of whether alternative energy sources can be developed in time to prevent an energy gap occurring if our supplies run out.

These environmental benefits are mostly of an essentially on-going nature and may in fact be expected to increase over time since Sections 2 and 3 indicated that a certain snowballing element determining the trends in trippages and container market shares is apparent. Thus a reduction in the returnables' market share means that fewer retailers will now be accepting returnables for the redemption of their deposit value. This makes it more difficult for consumers to return bottles, so trippage may fall. This will adversely affect the comparative costs of the returnable system resulting in a further reduction in their market share.

5.a.2. Economic Impact Costs

The economic impact costs, however, are not all of an on-going nature and it is important to make the distinction between short term structural adjustment costs and the long term permanent costs of a policy measure. In the policy selection process, an implicit or explicit trade off should be made between these transitional short term economic impacts and the ongoing long term economic and environmental impacts of a policy measure. It is useful to consider the determinants of the size of adjustment period and whether these adjustment costs could be reduced by an appropriate phasing-in of the policy measure which Quarles (US 20) stresses as an essential part of any policy programme.

The economic impact of a policy will be felt by consumers through changes in:
1. their convenience of consuming beverages;
2. the price of beverages.

The convenience to the individual consumer will be determined by the ease with which he is able to purchase beverages and then dispose of or return the container. Thus the policy will affect consumers through its effects on the availability of beverages in containers of the right size and right type (i.e. returnable or non-returnable).

As far as disposal is concerned, the non-returnable can, paper carton, plastic or glass bottle is more convenient than the returnable bottle which has to be returned to the retailer, and surveys (UK 4, US 2) show that the convenience value of the non-returnable container was the principal reason for the respondents' choice of the non-returnable bottle and can.

The value for this convenience obtained by purchasers of non-returnables can be estimated by comparing the price differential between the same beverage in a returnable and in a non-returnable container since economic theory of consumer behaviour says that this extra 'convenience' value that the consumer obtains from the non-returnable must be greater than this differential. If it were not, then he would have bought the beverage in a returnable bottle. However, there are some assumptions behind this economic theory which may not actually hold in the real world of the current market place.

First it is necessary that the consumer in choosing the non-returnable has a full range of choice of comparable returnable beverage bottles open to him. Many of the studies reviewed (CAN 1, US 17) mentioned the lack of full consumer choice or consumer sovereignty since in many shops and supermarkets beverages were frequently not available in returnable bottles. MRI (US 9) show the results of a survey which found that the proportion of respondents who said that returnable bottles were not available in their shops for beer was 47% and for soft drinks was 14%. Thus for these consumers the condition of full choice did not hold.

Second, the use of the net price differential* is not suitable where the consumer fails to perceive the deposit or where difficulty of reclaiming the deposit raises the real price to the consumer of a beverage in a returnable bottle. In these instances the use of the net price differential will overstate the convenience value of the non-returnable.

Thus it can be seen that it is difficult to estimate the convenience value on the basis of market data. An alternative method is to use the results of consumer surveys into what consumers are willing to pay for the convenience of non-returnables. The Dofasco survey quoted in CAN 1 showed that less than 3 ¢ was the maximum that more than 70% of consumers would be willing to pay for the convenience of a non-returnable container and 50% said that they would pay between 1 ¢ and 2 ¢. These results are subject to the problems of any survey that asks respondents for a monetary value. Another alternative method is to undertake a regression analysis of beverage sales before and after legislation was introduced. This analysis was used by US 38 to isolate the convenience factor from the other variables determining beverage sales in Vermont and Oregon. A value was then obtained for the consumers' convenience for non-returnables of, in Vermont, 2.3 ¢ for each beer container and 3.6 ¢ for each soft drink container and, in Oregon, 0.6 ¢ for each beer container and 0.8 ¢ for each soft drink container. It is notable that the Oregon legislation contained measures which made it easier for the consumer to return bottles. This suggests that the consumers' convenience value from non-returnables varies inversely with the inconvenience that he encounters in returning bottles

---

* The net price of a beverage in a returnable bottle is the full gross price of the beverage less the value of the deposit for the bottle.

for the redemption of their deposit value. Thus, despite the problems of its exact valuation, it can be said that some consumers do obtain some convenience value from non-returnable containers which will be reduced if measures are taken to curtail the market share of non-returnable containers, but that this loss of convenience will be lower if measures are taken to make it easier for consumers to return bottles.

The RTI survey (US 2) found that 36-48% of respondents chose returnable bottles for 'ecology remated' reasons. These consumers get welfare benefits from purchasing returnables in the form of 'feeling their doing something for the environment'. These consumers will then suffer welfare losses if their ability to purchase returnables is reduced and if the 'inconvenience' to them of returning bottles is increased and therefore any policy, which reduces the 'inconvenience' of returning bottles for refund, will yield benefits to this group.

The welfare of consumers will be affected by any change in beverage prices resulting from the policy. Table 5.1 shows the net price differential of beverages in returnable and non-returnable containers.

Table 5.1. A COMPARISON OF THE NET PRICE OF BEVERAGE IN RETURNABLE AND NON-RETURNABLE CONTAINERS

BEER - 1974 - $ PER CASE OF 24 x 12 oz. CONTAINERS

CONTAINER	AVERAGE PRICE PER CASE ($)
Returnable Bottle	5.46
Non-returnable Bottle	5.65
Metal Can	5.96

SOURCE: US 17.

These price differentials will vary between the different sectors of the beverage markets in the various countries depending upon the characteristics of the beverage market in each country. Section 3.a highlighted five variables determining the costs and price differentials of alternative beverage container systems. The most important of these was the trippage achieved by the returnable bottle, and the remaining determinants included the producers' markup, the container costs of the non-returnable, the extra labour costs of the returnable system and the transportation distances involved in the return process. Thus countries with relatively low transportation distances, due to high density of population, relatively low labour costs and high container costs (raw materials and energy), and experiencing high trippage values should have a bigger price differential in favour of returnable bottles.

The policy measure will affect the price of beverages through it impact on these variables, principally the trippage value, and through its impact on the containers' market shares. The size and direction of this impact on prices will be determined by the policy's effect on the actual prices of beverages in the alternative containers and the ensuing price differential between the containers whose market shares have risen or fallen.

The consumer will also be affected by any changes in tax rates due to the policy's impact on government revenue and expenditure.

The final resulting rise/fall in consumers' real disposable income will mean that the consumer will have more/less money to spend on goods and this will generate multiplier impacts on the national economy.

It is important to consider the economic dislocation of the policy on the internal costs, profits, employment, investment and capital stock levels of each sector of the beverage industry:
- Retailers
- Distributors
- Beverage manufactures (i.e. bottlers)
- Beverage container manufactures and their allied supply industries.

These impacts will result in changes in the total internal costs of beverage production and distribution and hence the final price of the beverage to the consumer. Thus the variations in the prices consumers pay for beverages, which have just been considered, will more or less summarize these impacts on the producers and sellers of beverages and beverage containers. Thus many of the economic impact studies (e.g. US 38) use the policies' impact on beverage prices as an effective summary indicator of the policies' effect on the beverage industry. However, consideration must also be given to a number of factors which result in the changes in beverage prices not being able to fully capture the economic impact caused by the policy measure. These are first that the beverage industry may not be able to pass increased costs into the consumer on account of the presence of government price controls. This will require an assessment of the policy's impacts on profit levels. Second, the policy may impose certain non-pecuniary costs on the beverage industry (e.g. strain on workers) which, in the short run at least may not show up the price changes and therefore may also merit separate consideration. Thirdly the policy may result in the obsolescence of certain capital equipment and this obsolescence will not show up in cost and price change if the producers follow a policy that 'byegones are byegones'. Thus although a producer would need to increase revenue to obtain a return on any additional new investment, he would not do so for obsolescent equipment which would be 'written off' as an irretrievable capital loss. Finally, it is frequently considered that the impacts on employment and investment are of sufficient importance to warrant special consideration in excess of the weights that have already been attached to these impacts through their inherent inclusion in the effect on beverage prices, e.g. by the producers raising prices so as to earn a return on extra investment as noted above.

5.a.2.1. The determinants of the size of economic impacts Costs

i) <u>Beverage sales level</u>. The size of the economic impacts will vary significantly with different levels of beverage consumption and a principal cause of the divergence of the various impact studies' results (US 2, US 11, US 9) is their differing assumptions over the behaviour of beverage sales. The policy will alter beverage consumption through its effect on beverage prices and consumer convenience which were considered earlier. Econometric models (US 2 and US 5) show that beverage consumption is relatively price inelastic and that it is not greatly affected by convenience packaging so that the impact of the policy on beverage consumption should not be great, although Weinberg (US 26) gives evidence to the contrary.

ii) <u>Changes in container market shares</u>. Each container requires different inputs of capital and labour from the various sectors of the beverage industry. Estimates of these inputs coefficients and the resulting impact on each sectors' profits can be gathered from information in the various impact studies (e.g. US 2, US 11, US 22, US 9) or from input/output tables. However, care must be taken in the interpretation of the input/output tables' coefficients since they do not take into account market imperfections (e.g. trade unions) or any flexibility in the production processes. Thus, for example, a shift in the container market shares from cans to returnable bottles will result in reduced labour and capital requirements in the can manufacturing sector which may not result in redundancies, due to the action of trade unions; the shift will increase the labour and capital requirements of bottlers and retailers but similarly may not result in increased employment and investment, due to productivity gains and increased overtime in these sectors, especially for small scale bottlers and retailers.

These economic impacts are important since the short term increase in investment required to adjust to the change in container shares, e.g. the investment in the float of returnable bottles and the changes in production and filling lines, uses up scarce capital resources while not actually increasing beverage production. Under-utilized and obsolescent capital represents a waste of resources as does unemployed labour which also creates a social problem and a drain on public funds through compensation and unemployment payments.

However, the above example shows that the total economic impact will be the net effect of employment losses in one sector offset against employment gains in another sector and it is important for the policy maker to evaluate the relative importance of these counteracting impacts.

5.a.2.2. The determinants of the importance of economic impacts

i) The nature of the capital market. If the sectors requiring increased investment, have difficulty in obtaining capital funds then it may be necessary for the government to step in with short term loans to avert the threat of bankruptcy.

ii) The nature of the labour market. The losses in employment levels will cause severe social hardships if the unemployment is concentrated in certain regions and in areas of the labour market where the chances of getting another job are low so that the unemployed can expect to remain unemployed longer. This will be determined not only by the national economic situation but also by the regional concentration of the affected sector and the skills of the unemployed which determine their potential for finding a new job. The gains in employment will cause problems if there is a shortage of labour for this type of work but will reap benefits if there is unemployed labour available. Generally the container manufacturing and their allied supply sectors are more regionally concentrated and so there is a potential regional unemployment problem if the container manufacturing sector is adversely affected. However, jobs in this sector will be more skilled than the jobs affected in the retail and bottling sectors. Therefore, it is important to analyse the labour market situation of each affected category of labour. Generally there is lower unemployment and greater demand for skilled workers than for unskilled workers with no ticket to sell on the market, and therefore any job gains and losses in the retailing and bottling sector will be relatively more important than job gains or losses in the container manufacturing sector. Although this situation does not hold in some countries (e.g. the Netherlands) where there is a shortage of unskilled labour.

iii) Current container market shares. If one uses the above example again of a shift from cans to returnable bottles, then the impact of the shift will be determined by the dependance of the container manufacturers on sales to the beverage industry. This will be a function of the current container market shares for the can or other affected containers and the degree of specialization or diversity of the container manufacturer. Thus if, prior to the policy change, the can held a large share of the beverage market and these cans were produced by specialized container manufacturers who only produced beverage cans, then the policy would have a large impact on this sector.

However, favourable economic impacts and the potential for environmental improvement (e.g. litter and solid waste reductions) also depend upon the size of the can's market share which can be replaced by returnable bottles and thus there is a direct trade off between the favourable and unfavourable effects of a policy and it is necessary to see if there is an alternative method of achieving the environmental benefit while reducing the adverse economic impacts (e.g. recycling and anti-litter campaigns, see Sections 5.h and 5.j) and whether there is potential for alleviating those adverse economic impacts which are principally of a short term dislocation nature.

5.a.2.3. Means to alleviate the adverse economic impacts

The adverse economic impacts of underutilized capital and unemployed labour in the beverage industry could be eased by natural market forces. This slack in the beverage industry could be taken up by increased production due to expanding foreign sales and overall increases in the size of the market. Table 5.2 shows an American forecast of employment projections in beverage related industries which indicates that the expected growth in the retail and packaging sector should mitigate any employment losses in these sectors with the exception of the aluminium fabrication sector, although these forecasts are based on the existing market structure and therefore do not take account of any possible reduction in total sales as a result of policies which might raise the price of certain beverage products. A similar picture may be expected to emerge for other countries.

The natural wastage or turnover rates will determine the ability of the various sectors to withstand the economic impacts without having to declare redundancies. These turnover rates will depend upon the general economic situation and the profile of the industry (i.e. are the jobs of a transient nature as in the retail trade or of a more permanent nature as in can manufacture). Estimates of the turnover rates are 2% per month for the glass bottle industry, 1% per month for the metal container industry (US 11) and 5% for the brewing industry (US 13).

Table 5.2. EMPLOYMENT PROJECTIONS IN INDUSTRIES RELATED TO BEVERAGE CONTAINER PRODUCTION

INDUSTRY	EMPLOYMENT INCREASE FORECAST ('000's)	
	1972-80	1980-85
Glass	50	11
Aluminium rolling and drawing	-9	0
Metal containers	+6	0
Misc. metal products	+15	10
Other fab. metal products	174	49
Wholesale trade	736	177
Retail trade	2,514	536

SOURCE: US 25.

Government action will help to alleviate the adverse economic impacts. The policy maker can use these natural market forces to reduce the dislocation impact by a gradual phasing-in of the policy. It is important to recognize, in the policy formulation stage, the problems that this phasing-in may cause so that these problems can, where possible, be overcome and a choice made of the suitable phasing-in procedure so that the policy's economic impact cost can be minimized. Generally, it is easier to phase-in taxes, which can be gradually raised to their desired level, than regulatory measures such as mandatory deposits, ban or standardization. Although the policy could include provisions for a transition period of 'n' years/months before mandatory deposits, a ban or standardization was fully implemented. This would considerably reduce the transitional economic dislocation that might otherwise be caused by these measures. EPA shows that a phasing-in of mandatory deposit legislation over a 5 year period would reduce the employment dislocations (e.g. redundancies) by 32% (US 1, US 20). However, as MRI (US 9) point out, there must be certainty over the provision for the phasing-in and the ultimate implementation of the policy if industry is to be induced to take the necessary steps to alleviate the economic impacts of the policy.

The government could also use its regional industrial policy and job training schemes to ease the transitional economic impact of the policy.

5.a.3. The Impact of the Policy on the Government Sector

It will be evident so far that the policy measure will affect public finances through its impact on government expenditure for:

i) solid waste and litter collection and disposal;
ii) unemployment and compensation expenditures paid to workers laid off by the policy; this will depend on the current rates of unemployment payments and the time that the workers spend on the unemployment register;
iii) expenditures for job training, regional and industrial aid (e.g. investment grants, loans etc.) that are directly related to the policy.

Government revenue will rise/fall depending upon the size of:

iv) any tax revenue that the policy measure will yield;
v) the rise/fall in beverage consumption, especially beer, which leads to a rise/fall in excise tax revenue;
vi) the change in corporation tax revenue due to the change in the beverage industry's profit levels and increases in its depreciation and capital write-off allowances due to the obsolescence of current capital and, the extra investment requirements resulting from the policy;
vii) any change in income tax that results from the change in labour earnings caused by the policy.

This change in labour earnings is the change in employment times the wage rate of each affected labour category. The labour earnings related to the non-returnable containers are higher than for the returnable bottle and therefore any move to returnables will lower the average earnings rates in the beverage industry which will compound or offset the effect of the fall or rise in numbers employed on labour earnings.

(ii)-(vii) will be increased by any multiplier effects on the national economy of the economic impact on the beverage industry and the change in consumers disposable income resulting from the policy. The size of the multiplier effect will be determined by the size and direction of the economic impact of the policy, and the importance of the beverage related industries in the national economy. This will be reflected in their multiplier coefficients which MRI gives American estimates for (US 9).

Thus the public sector finances will be considerably affected by the policy measure. But, when undertaking an overall appraisal of a policy, it is necessary to avoid double counting since many of these effects are income transfers to sectors that have already been considered in the economic impact evaluation. For example, unemployment payments and capital write-offs were considered in the previous section.

Further criteria for evaluating a policy measure are:
1. administrative feasibility and the cost of a policy which will be determined by the policy's use of market forces or government regulation;
2. the international trade implications;
3. the impact on the competitive structure of the beverage industry which will depend upon the impact of the policy on the number of firms entering and leaving the industry and any changes in the leading firms' market shares;
4. the impacts on the balance of payments;
5. the policy's impact on technological change and innovation; this is considered separately in section 5.k;
6. political acceptability of the policy, which will depend principally upon the expected and publicized impact of the measure on prices, jobs and environmental benefits.

This political acceptability should be estimated by surveys into consumer attitudes on the policy measures rather than interpretation of consumer opinion from their market choice between alternative beverage containers, on account of what Lidgren (SWE 5) calls the opinion paradox. This basically relates to the free rider nature of the issue since the convenience value of the container is obtained by each consumer individually while the environmental benefits are spread over all society. This means that a consumer may well buy a convenience non-returnable container but paradoxically support policy measures (e.g. a ban) against non-returnables since his convenient value from the non-returnable will be greater than the environmental benefits, to him, of his not buying a non-returnable but, may be less than the environmental benefits if everyone else also does not buy a non-returnable.

5.b. The Non-Intervention Policy

It may seem that the above analysis assumes that the government undertakes a policy towards the beverage container. This is logical if one extends the definition of policy to include the policy of not intervening in the market - a 'No Action' policy. Such a policy will be justified if the external benefits of returnables are not significant enough to cover the economic dislocation and administrative costs of a policy favouring returnables. Although the 'No Action' option does not involve any actual government intervention, adjustments in the beverage industry will still continuously be made in the face of 'unregulated' market forces. It is difficult to predict exactly the size of these adjustments but an indication can be ascertained from current forecasts and an extrapolation of past trends.

If one takes the UK as an example, Table 2.3 in Section 2 shows that over the past five years the returnable bottle's share of the beer and soft drink market has fallen by 18 percentage points while the shares of non-returnable bottles and cans have risen by 5 and 13 percentage points respectively. Metal Box (UK 17) estimate that in 1979 the returnable bottle's share will fall by a further 12 percentage points to 54% while the non-returnable bottle and the metal can will rise by 2 and 10 percentage points to 12 and 34% respectively.

Table 3.5 in Section 3 shows the recent decline that has occurred in trippage in America and a similar picture is apparent in the UK (UK 4, UK 17), so that by 1979/80 trippage in the UK might be expected, in the absence of government intervention, to fall for soft drinks from 9.0 to about 6.5 and for beer from 13.4 to about 10.

During the past two decades there have been strong trends of increasing centralization and specialization in the beverage industry in both USA and UK. Unfortunately, actual figures are not available for the UK; but in the USA the number of soft drinks bottling plants fell from 6,662 in 1950 to 2,692 in 1973 despite a sales increase over this period of 276%. Most of these plant reductions have been in the small local firms and the market share of the 20 largest companies has increased from 20% to 32% (US 12). Similarly, an increase in concentration has occurred in the UK brewing industry (UK 32).

The previous analysis shows that the decline in trippage and the trend towards non-returnables will result in environmental costs in the form of increased litter, solid waste and energy consumption. The energy requirements of the alternative beverage containers is forecast to be reduced overtime by technological innovations that will occur in the absence of any beverage container legislation, on account of increase in the internal cost of energy. The increase in the market share of non-returnable containers will raise the profits, investment and employment levels in the container manufacturing sector. However, the Quebec Soft Drink Association (CAN 2) state that the continuation of current trends would also result in the closure of many labour intensive regional bottlers; the resulting employment losses will cause problems in these regions and may exceed the employment gains which will occur in the more capital intensive and centralized sectors of the beverage industry.

A change in market shares from returnables to non-returnables will mean that consumers will benefit from the increased convenience attached to non-returnables, but will suffer from the increased 'inconvenience' of returning bottles in a smaller market. Beverage prices will rise on account of the increased costs of the returnable system due to the fall in trippage and the increased transportation distances resulting from the greater centralization in the beverage industry. The price of non-returnables will rise on account of increased raw material and energy prices leading to greater container and transportation costs. Stern (US 17) quotes brewers' forecasts, from the Wall Street Journal, of rising container costs and suggests that this will be greater than the rise in labour costs. A view supported by EPA's figures (US 1 - based on industry estimates) which show that can prices rose by 34% during 1974 while returnable glass bottles rose by only 16% so that the price differential of beverages in cans and returnable bottles was widened. Although 1974 is not considered to be a typical year (UK 31) yet data from Ontario for 1975 (CAN 3) shows a similar trend.

The above position relates to the policy 'off' situation. We do not profess to any accuracy in crystal ball gazing but hope that we have given a good general, albeit not precise, impression of what can be expected to occur in the absence of government intervention. These policy 'off' impacts must be used as a baseline against which the impacts of any other policy measure must be compared and the above analysis effectively highlights the essential dynamic nature of our current economic system which means that as the economic situation changes then it is inevitable and desirable that a certain structural reallocation of the economy should occur. What must be considered is whether the economic and environmental impacts that result from the free market induced structural change are preferable to the impacts of the government policy induced structural changes.

We shall now review the impacts of the various policy options on the basis of various impact studies that have been undertaken. These studies are based on both hypothetical data and actual legislative experiences. We stress that these studies do not predict exactly what would happen if another country introduced the same policy measures, for reasons given earlier, but they do yield good information on the effects of each policy and should give a useful impression of what might be expected to occur.

There is considerable controversy over these impact studies, particularly in the case of the Oregon legislation. Unfortunately it is not possible in a report of this scope to give a critical and detailed evaluation of the assumptions and calculations behind each study's result so that Sections 5.c-g will just briefly summarize the various impact studies' results and assumptions.

5.c.   Ban on All Non-Refillable Containers

A ban on all non-refillable containers is a popular and frequently cited policy proposal. This is because the legislation is relatively easy to enforce and the results are obvious.

However, there are few instances in which an outright ban has been implemented; normally this policy has been combined with some other policy option. The reason this is necessary is to ensure that the policy will create the desired effect, that is to reduce environmental impacts. As it stands, an outright ban of non-refillable containers will not guarantee that the substitute - a completely refillable system - will generate the right incentives to ensure that containers are returned. Thus, as in the case of the Oregon Bottle Bill, a ban on pull-top cans has been combined with a refund system for refillables. In Norway the high tax on cans has in effect amounted to a ban, but this is a different approach because the removal of cans from the beverage container market has been achieved through the market mechanism and is therefore an incentive policy. In Denmark a ban has been implemented to maintain the status quo of the present market shares for carbonated soft drinks and mineral water (i.e. to prevent the can taking a significant share of the market). A ban, however, is a restrictive policy.

Because empirical data is unavailable two theoretical studies (US 9 and US 11) have been used as information basis.

The Midwest Research Institute (US 9) has studied the impacts of a ban on non-refillable container for the USA. Their conclusions suggest that a ban would incur negative impact costs of $ 10 billion, and benefits less than half this amount. The major findings of this report were:
  i) Sales decline of 8% due to loss of consumer convenience, reductions in the number of outlets and brands inventoried.
  ii) Net loss of 10,000 jobs. Losses of 66,000 jobs in steel, metal can and glass industries but increase of 56,000 jobs in beverage production, distribution and retailing. The jobs lost would, in general, be higher paid skilled jobs, whereas, jobs gained would be more manual.
  iii) The major benefits would be less than 50% of the $ 10 billion costs. Specifically, external benefits would include a decrease in littering of 11.3% and reductions in solid waste of 1.37%.

Folk (US 11) estimates the following impacts for Minnesota:
- i) No change in sales.
- ii) Employment gains of 2.327 jobs compared with losses of 1.658 jobs - a net gain of 669 jobs.
- iii) Consumer savings of $ 18 million (due to lower prices of beverage in refillable containers), which in turn, when spent elsewhere, would generate an estimated further 1.200 jobs.

It is clear that there are large discrepancies between the two sets of results and these largely result from two assumptions. Firstly, the sales decline of 8% (MRI estimate) will substantially increase the costs of moving to a refillable system. This figure is the industry consensus which MRI used; they disregarded the 1-2% sales decline which was obtained by them from a consumer survey (US 9). Secondly, the assumption by MRI that trippage will fall from 18.5 for beer and 12.5 for soft drink to 8 in both industries assumes that there is no improvement in the ease of return, a critical factor in trippage. Furthermore, if bottlers desire to get their bottles back they would doubtless provide further incentives such as higher deposit rates. Higher trippage values would increase the benefits of a refillable system.

In a similar report by EPA (US 3) where the impacts of mandatory deposits are used to effect a ban, the consumption or sales of beverages is assumed to fall by 4%. While the effects of a ban are far from clear it is apparent that such a policy would amount to large dislocation impacts (SWE 4) which are likely to be greater than the environmental benefits, and it would be necessary to include further legislation to create incentives for increasing return rates by higher deposits and improving customer's ease of return. These options are more fully discussed below (see Sections 5.d, 5.e and 5.i).

5.d. Mandatory Deposits on Beverage Containers

Under this approach a mandatory deposit is required on all beverage containers. Deposits have historically been the incentive used by producers of beverage containers to achieve economically viable returnable systems. The objective of a mandatory deposit is to create a minimum value on all containers, which would encourage their return by the consumer.

One of the most important considerations for a mandatory deposit is the level at which the minimum deposit is set. If it is set too high, consumption will be discouraged and, furthermore it may become cheaper for the bottler to buy a new bottle rather than redeem the deposit on a used bottle. While the bottler may be obliged by the law to redeem the deposit he may make return inconvenient in order to reduce the number of bottles returned, and this is particularly relevant where trippage is related to ease of return, rather than the size of the deposit. The deposit should be set low enough so as to create an incentive for beverage manufacturers to get their bottles returned and make the inconvenience of return as small as possible. If the deposit is too small, however, then there will be a lower return rate from consumers than expected and the bottler may well suffer losses due to excessive replacement costs. It should also be noted that a mandatory deposit legislation usually contains measures to ensure that all retailers are required to refund these deposits on all beverage containers of the type they sell. One problem that may be associated with mandatory deposit legislation, and that must be taken into account, is the effect on certain small retailers of receiving a disproportionate number of returned bottles.

Section 3.a showed the net price of beverage to be lower in refillable bottles than non-refillable bottles and cans. If a deposit must be paid on all beverage containers, it is likely that consumers will switch to a refillable system because, if they are going to return the container to redeem the deposit, then they will buy the cheapest container available. Thus most of the studies suggest that, as a result of mandatory deposit legislation, the non-refillable bottle will disappear. The metal can, however, will maintain a certain, perhaps reduced, share of the market on account of consumer willingness to pay extra for the beverage in a can and, as Section 3.a showed, there may be instances of low trippage and high transport distances which make the can a cheaper container. Thus RTI develop two scenarios (see later) which involve different assumptions on the sensitivity of the metal can market to the deposit.

Table 5.3 shows the conflicting results of three studies into the impacts on the total systems costs of beverages of a major shift from throwaway to refillable bottles. The reason for the divergence is the different values used by each study for the important components of total systems costs mentioned in Section 3.a. Folk (US 11) gives further evidence to support the view that mandatory deposit legislation would result in a reduction in costs and beverage prices if it is passed on to consumers (this will be determined by the level of competition in the beverage market). Folk estimates, in his study of the impacts of mandatory deposits in Illinois, that this reduction in prices will result in savings to consumers amounting to $ 71 million.

However, the consumer although he gains through this reduction in his expenditures, will lose the convenience value he attaches to non-returnable containers or lose his forfeited deposit should he fail to return the container. EPA (US 3) estimates the price differential between refillable and non-refillable containers to be 1 ¢ for beer and 2 ¢ for soft drinks, which yielded a total expenditure in 1969 for convenience of $ 598.4 million. There are considerable problems involved in calculating this important, but difficult, cost and, as was shown in Section 5.a, it is also necessary to consider the existence of full consumer choice between refillable and non-refillable and the impacts of mandatory legislation on reducing the inconvenience of returning containers, since now retailers will be required to redeem deposits for all containers of the type that they sell.

Table 5.3. COST IMPACTS OF SWITCHING FROM EXISTING CONTAINER SYSTEMS TO REFILLABLE SYSTEMS
$ per case of 12 oz. containers*

STUDY	BEVERAGE	CONTAINER MARKET SHARE SHIFT	CHANGE IN TOTAL SYSTEM COST, $
Weinberg (US 26)	Beer	Complete shift from existing mix to refillable bottles	+0.46
Faucett (US 27)	Beer	Shift to refillable bottles from cans	-0.08
	Beer	Shift to refillable bottles from non-returnable bottles	-0.00
	Soft drinks	Shift to refillable bottles from cans	-0.31
	Soft drinks	Shift to refillable bottles from non-returnable bottles	-0.33
RTI (US 2) ..	Beer and Soft drinks	Shift from existing mix to predicted mix	-0.12

* Assumes a trippage of 10.
SOURCE: US 2, US 26, US 27.

The impact upon consumption or sales of beverages due to mandatory deposits is the subject of some debate. The American industry (US 26) is of the opinion that the recent rapid growth of sales for both beer and soft drinks is a direct result of the 'convenience package'. Thus any legislation will have a severe impact upon consumption if the use of such packages is restricted. However, the convenience of the package is an insignificant determinant of beverage consumption according to statistical analysis of regression equations (US 5) which shows that the major variables are personal disposable income, age distribution of population, and the relative price of beverage. Most studies carried out for the Federal Government assume no significant decline in sales as a result of mandatory 5 ¢ deposit legislation. The EPA (US 3) has assumed a 4% decline in sales with a high mandatory deposit of 10 ¢ per container and Folk (US 11) assumes that the imposition of mandatory deposit legislation will cause no change in the level of beverage consumption. This evidence suggests that any decline in sales will be small, but this is dependent upon the size of the deposit and the percentage share of the non-returnable in the beverage container market.

One of the major costs of a move to a refillable system as a result of mandatory deposits will be the change in capital requirements. Two costs may be separated. Firstly, the costs of writing-off present machinery and, secondly, the necessary new investment required for an all refillable system. While the impacts will depend upon the length of time over which the new legislation is enacted, estimates of costs have been made by both EPA (US 3) and RTI (US 2).

RTI use two scenarios. The first assumes that cans maintain their 1976 market share through to 1982; this requires additional capital requirement of $ 824 million. In the second scenario, where cans lose half their market share, the capital requirement will be $ 2,006 million. This investment includes the impacts upon indirect and direct industries. In both scenarios, it is assumed that the non-refillable bottle disappears completely from the beverage container market.

EPA suggest that the impact of a 10 ¢ deposit, on capital, had legislation been enacted in 1969, would have approached $ 2,529 million. This includes $ 1,361 million in capital write-offs and $ 1,168 million additional investment requirements. Compared to the 5 ¢ deposit, the 10 ¢ deposit has a larger capital impact due to the higher deposit level and the 4% anticipated sales decline.

Employment impacts of mandatory deposit legislation are detailed at length by the Research Triangle Institute (US 2). These are summarized in Table 5.4.

Two main impacts are discernable from Table 5.4. Employment and earnings will have a net positive gain due to deposit legislation, but the new jobs will be less skilled and thus lower paid. However, this transition from skilled to unskilled labour may be seen as beneficial where chronic unemployment is greatest amongst unskilled workers; this is the case in some countries.

The benefits of a mandatory deposit legislation comprise the environmental gains accruing from decreases in litter and solid waste generation plus decreases in material usage, water pollution, air pollution and energy consumption. The Stanford Research Institute (US 29) gives the savings in material inputs and pollution outputs as summarized in Table 5.5.

The switch from non-returnable bottles and cans to refillable bottles will result in savings in municipal solid waste of the order of 5-6 million tonnes (US 28) implying reductions in solid waste disposal costs of $ 110 million, in 1972 figures, although this amount includes

Table 5.4. PROBABLE EMPLOYMENT IMPACTS
OF MANDATORY DEPOSIT LEGISLATION

	NET LABOUR REQUIREMENTS (000's)	EARNINGS 10^6 $	WAGE LEVELS $/ANNUM
Containers:			
Glass	-12.4	-118	10,640
Cans	-20.4	-231	"
Metal manufacture	-8.3	-97	11,687
Beverage production	-16.6	-134	8,072
Distribution	+45.1	+556	12,328
Retailing	+89.5	+624	6,792
Indirect industries	-42.6	-355	8,333
Net total	+34.3	+244	
Average			7,113

SOURCE: US 2.

savings in collection costs which may not become apparent for some time (see Section 4.b on waste disposal).

Mandatory deposits will have two, possibly conflicting, impacts on the level of recycling undertaken. Firstly, this change in the level and composition of solid waste may adversely affect the viability of one alternative method of solid waste management - the operation of resource recovery facilities. RTI (US 2) estimates that the reduction in the glass and metallic content of solid waste, following mandatory deposit legislation, will result in a 19% decline in the revenue potential from separating these materials which may mean that recycling these materials is no longer profitable. However RTI states that this would not alter the decision to install a resource recovery system except in marginal economic circumstances. This view is supported by the opinions of experts in this field that the viability of resource recovery systems is determined more by the capital costs and the costs of alternative disposal methods than the glass and metallic content of solid waste. This is especially true for the currently popular energy recovery systems for which the paper and combustible component is very much more important than the glass and metallic content. In fact it is shown (US 38) that mandatory deposit legislation would raise

Table 5.5. MATERIAL INPUTS AND POLLUTION OUTPUTS
(per million litres in 12 oz. containers)

	MARKET SHARES OF RETURNABLE AND NON-RETURNABLE CONTAINERS		% CHANGE
	EXISTING MIX	MIX PREDICTED WITH MANDATORY DEPOSITS	
Materials	1,807 tonnes	624 tonnes	-65%
Water inputs ...	15,950,000 litres	7,320,000 litres	-54%
Air pollutants ..	40,098 tonnes	22,630 tonnes	-44%
Water pollutants	71,830 kg	14,260 kg	-80%
Process solid waste	390 tonnes	114 tonnes	-71%

SOURCE: US 29.

the profitability of the Maryland steam recovery plant since it would increase the combustible portion of solid waste that would be treated at the plant. Secondly, mandatory deposit legislation will result in the return of non-refillable bottles and cans, for redemption of their deposits. This will provide a mechanism for the recycling of these containers although in some instances, where there is no recycling market available, the returned containers may end up on the landfill site.

Energy savings are estimated for the USA by RTI (US 2) under the two scenarios described above. Scenario 1 suggests a reduction of 168×10^{16} therms of energy and there is a reduction of 144×10^{16} therms of energy under scenario 2. In Europe, however, these savings may well be less due to the dearth of the aluminium can.

Most of the benefits summarized so far are relatively small and can be expected to have no more than a marginal impact. A beneficial impact of mandatory legislation, however, is expected to occur with a decrease in the level of litter and littering. Firstly, mandatory deposits will induce consumers to return containers because if they do not they will incur a direct penalty equal to the value of the refund. This aspect of mandatory deposit legislation has a great deal of conceptual appeal because the policy has a direct impact upon the cause of the problem. The litterbug, the individual who has created the external cost, will under mandatory deposit legislation be forced to pay for this action; hence the policy goes a long way towards internalizing the external costs. Secondly, any containers that are, nevertheless, littered will have a value equal to the level of the deposit. This will induce scavenging by people who are prepared to collect these containers and claim the refund, reducing further the level of litter.

Quantification of the benefits of decreased littering is extremely difficult due to the problem of assessing the aesthetic losses associated with litter and most studies only consider the savings in litter collection costs as a minimum surrogate for the social cost of litter. If all beverage container litter is eliminated then a litter collection cost saving of $ 98 million for the USA in 1976 prices has been estimated by EPA (US 3). This assumes that 25% of all litter is beverage container related. The only empirical data available comes from Oregon, where the primary concern of the policy was the level of littering due to beverage containers; because of the direct nature of mandatory deposit legislation upon the litterbug, a mandatory deposit policy was adopted. This is more fully discussed in Section 5.e on the Oregon Experience (see also Section 4.c on litter).

The success of mandatory deposit legislation will depend upon customer and retailer support for the policy. Stern quotes the ADS study's results (US 30), which show that 91% of the respondents signified approval of the Oregon Bottle Bill and many desired an extension of the scope of the legislation to cover other items (US 17). However, MRI (US 9) show that popular support is not as great for mandatory deposits as it is for a ban and in some American states (e.g. Washington) the public has voted against mandatory deposit legislation. This is due to fears of adverse economic impacts and also the consumers' dissatisfaction with returning non-refillable cans which are at best recycled but frequently just thrown out by the retailers (CAN 1). The scrap value of a non-refillable container is estimated to be only about .75 ȼ while the extra cost of handling the returned container is estimated to be about .4 ȼ (US 17) so that each time a retailer redeems a 5 ȼ deposit container he will fail to gain about 4.65 ȼ and this means that it will be in the retailers' interest to discourage the return of cans. This raises administrative problems of enforcing the mandatory legislation so that retailers accept returned containers and it was for reasons of administrative difficulties that Sweden rejected a general policy of mandatory deposits (SWE 4), although it has been recommended that wine and spirits containers should carry a minimum deposit. The reason that these containers have been singled out is the state monopoly control of wines and spirits retailing, which overcomes the administrative difficulties of a mandatory deposit.

In the absence of a state controlled monopoly, the administrative problems could be eased if the deposit was set low enough so that the retailers and distributors were encouraged rather than compelled to accept returnable bottles. However, the deposit could not be set low enough to encourage the acceptance of returned cans and another alternative is the setting up of special recycling collection depots, as has occurred in Alberta (CAN 1), but this entails extra costs for the running of the depots and requires consumers to make a special trip, outside their normal shopping routine, to return the container.

An alternative to the mandatory imposition of deposits on all
containers is the system of refillable bottles which do not bear a deposit,
but are purchased by independent dealers at their resource value, as a
new bottle. These dealers then sell the bottles to bottle merchants
who sell them back to the bottlers. This system operates, with apparent
success, in certain Australian states where a trippage of 5-7 is achieved
(AUS 2). The advantages of this system is that it does not have to operate
though the retail network and therefore would involve less disruption of
the beverage industry. The system could also be extended to cover other
containers, for which the ordinary deposit - return system may not be
appropriate and the resource value paid for the bottle could be raised
to allow for the greater cost of returning bottles from distant markets.
This aspect is, of course, particularly relevant to a large and sparsely
populated country like Australia. However discussion of this system
with various interested parties revealed that it has many disadvantages.
The principal purpose of mandatory deposit legislation is to intervene
in the beverage market so that the marketing position of the returnable
bottle and the consumers' ease of returning bottles are improved e.g.
by creating certainty that he will be able to return his bottle easily for
a set deposit. In contrast this alternative system could seriously impair the consumers ease of returning bottles since the re-purchasing
process is not necessarily an integral part of the normal retail distribution system and hence may be outside the normal shopping pattern.
Furthermore, this separate return system through dealers and bottle
merchants will incur extra costs which will lower the size of the deposit
that the dealer can offer. Thus in South Australia dealers were only
paying consumers 0.5 ¢ for each returned bottle. This along with the
consumers uncertainty as to the actual sum of the resource value for
the bottle, will reduce the consumers willingness to return bottles.
Thus it is felt that, in many other countries, consumers and the bottlers
would prefer the ordinary deposit system to this alternative of purchasing
non-deposit bottles at their resource value.

Such a repurchasing system also operated for wines and spirits
bottles in Norway where the national wine monopoly paid N.Kr 0.40
for each domestic wine and spirit bottle returned. However, this system currently achieves a trippage of only 1.8-3.4. This is attributed to,
among other things, the low price offered for the returned bottles (NOR 1).
The same study goes on to say that considerable benefits would be gained
by replacing this repurchasing system by a uniform mandatory deposit
system which it predicts would increase the return rate significantly.
It also states that the implementation of a mandatory deposit would result
in economic impacts and some transitional problems for the wine monopoly, but that it is nevertheless expected that the problems will be overcome in a reasonable manner.

5.e. Oregon Type Legislation

Discussion of the impacts of a ban and mandatory deposit legislation in the two preceding sections has shown that while both methods generate certain environmental benefits, they may have large dislocation impacts on the industry. Bans, while effective, have the greatest impact on industry and mandatory deposits, which have smaller dislocation impacts, will not guarantee that the metal can (particularly the ring-pull type) will be successfully prevented from maintaining its market share and hence its impact on litter. Certain policies have therefore been designed that combine these two measures in an attempt to derive their maximum benefits while avoiding the greatest costs. The Oregon experience is the most well documented.

The Oregon Bottle Bill was introduced in 1972 with the objective of reducing the beverage container component of litter. The legislation required that all beverage containers carry a refundable value of at least 5 ¢ (or 2 ¢ in the case of a registered standard container). The sale of all beverage cans with detachable parts, e.g. "ring-tabs" and "pull-tabs" for easy opening, was prohibited.

Subsequent consideration of the legislation has emphasized other environmental benefits which have been realized. For example, a decrease in household solid waste which will reduce the burden on local municipalities, a decrease in the raw material requirements and hence less quarrying and mining, and finally a decrease in the use of energy.

The legislation appears very successful in reducing roadside litter. Despite difficulties in measuring litter (see Section 4.c) the following results were observed:
1. the number of beverage containers littered per mile of road per month decreased from 127 to 43;
2. beverage related litter fell from 30% of total pieces to 11%;
3. measured by volume, beverage container litter declined from 43% of total litter to 19%.

This reduction was achieved despite a general upward trend in littering, hence the estimates shown above are likely to understate the impacts of the legislation. The present bulk of roadside litter (90%) is non-beverage related and is unaffected by the legislation.

Household solid waste is estimated to have decreased 4-5% by weight. This suggests a decrease of some 80-90% of beverage containers entering the solid waste stream. While the short run impacts will show a decline in solid waste management costs of 1% (disposal savings), in the long run savings may increase to the full 5% (disposal + collection). Energy savings are roughly estimated at 56% of initial energy requirements (US 4).

These environmental benefits are due to the market impact of the legislation on container market shares and return rates shown in Tables 5.6 and 5.7.

Table 5.6. CHANGES IN CONTAINER MARKET SHARES IN OREGON

% OF CONTAINERS WHICH WERE	12 MONTHS PRIOR TO IMPLEMENTATION OF BILL	12 MONTHS AFTER IMPLEMENTATION OF BILL
Returnable Bottles		
Beer	31	96
Soft Drinks	53	88
Cans		
Beer	40	3
Soft Drinks	40	12

SOURCE US 4.

Table 5.7. CHANGES IN RETURN RATES IN OREGON FOLLOWING THE BILL

RETURNABLE BOTTLE/ BEVERAGE	12 MONTHS PRIOR TO IMPLEMENTATION OF BILL	12 MONTHS AFTER IMPLEMENTATION OF BILL
Non-standard		
Beer	75%	90%
Soft Drinks	80%	92%
Standard		
Beer	75%	95%

SOURCE: US 4.

Table 5.7 shows the increase in return rates (hence in trippage) as a result of the Oregon Bottle Bill. The combined effects, shown in Tables 5.6 and 5.7, have meant a considerable savings in materials. Very large reductions in the use of aluminium and steel were expected, but it is interesting to note that less glass was also required after implementation of the bill.

The success of the Oregon legislation is mainly attributable to resultant high return rates that have been achieved. This is due in the main to the ease with which consumers are able to return their used containers. The system of lower deposits for 'certified standard bottles' indicates that the ease of return is of greater importance than the size of the deposit for increasing return rates (this aspect of the Oregon

Bottle Bill is further explained in Section 5.i: Standardisation of beverage containers, below).

There has been a discernible change in retail prices following the bill. In fact consumers now pay slightly less in total for the same volume of beverages than would have been the case under the pre-Bottle Bill conditions.

Consumption of beverages has not declined as a result of the legislation and, although the rate of growth of beer sales decreased in 1973, the year of transition, this was in line with the national experiences for that year.

Employment effects have proved positive with a net increase of 365 full-yime jobs and a net labour earnings increase of $ 1.6 million. The tendency for the loss of skilled jobs for unskilled ones is also apparent.

Capital losses were negligible largely because the legislation covers only Oregon and existing equipment could be transferred to supply neighbouring markets. The shift to the refillable system resulted in an increase in capital investment requirements of $ 3.2 million in-plant and equipment and $ 1.6 million in bottle stock (US 4), and the great proportion of this total was undertaken in the first year following the bill.

Gudger and Walters (US 14) show that the bill resulted in a $ 16.5 million increase in the beverage industry's operating income which results from the savings in container costs for brewers and soft drink bottlers due to greater use of refillable bottles. But these cost savings have to be offset against the container manufacturers' lost profit and the increased costs of the returnable system for the beverage manufacturers, distributors and retailers. Gudger and Walters estimate these extra costs total $ 12.5 million, yielding a net increase in operating income of $ 3.9 million. On the contrary, the ADS study (US 30), quoted in US 22, shows a net decrease in operating income of between $ 6.9-8.6 million. The reason for the discrepancy between these two results is the lower return rates used in the ADS study, which means that the container cost savings figure is lower. This again signifies the importance of trippage to the success of a policy measure.

5.f. A High Tax on All Beverage Containers

The policy measures considered so far have all been of a regulatory nature with the government imposing a ban on all non-returnable containers (Section 5.c) or requiring that all beverage containers should carry a mandatory deposit (Section 5.d) or a combination of the two - Oregon (Section 5.e). However, the beverage container problem can also be approached by the use of market incentives through the levying of taxes on all beverage containers. There are three possible variations of this approach: the first is a high or medium tax on beverage containers (Section 5.f), the second is a product charge on all packaging products (Section 5.g) and the third is a low litter tax on beverage containers (Section 5.h) which is designed not to yield environmental benefits, through adjustments in the container market shares, but to raise revenue which can be used to finance an anti-litter campaign and hence reduce the social costs of litter.

The taxation approach has considerable conceptual appeal since it means that it can be set at a level so that the beverage containers will now cover their social (external) costs and thus it accords with the polluter pays principle. Also the tax will encourage the returnable beverage container.

The mechanism by which this will work can best be seen in the example of a tax of 5 ¢ levied on all beverage containers produced. A non-returnable container will bear the full amount (5 ¢) of the tax but the refillable container will have the advantage of spreading the tax over the number of trips made by each container. Thus, if the trippage is say, 10, then the increased cost for each beverage solid in a returnable will be only .5 ¢, and therefore the price differential of beverages will have moved in favour of returnables by 4.5 ¢ so that their market share will rise. However, this widening of the price differential will depend upon the trippage achieved by the returnable bottle and Section 4 showed that the social benefits of the returnable bottle also depend upon the trippage achieved. Therefore the taxation policy will use market forces to encourage the returnable beverage container precisely where its its trippage will yield greatest social benefits. This will be more efficient than the blanket use of a regulatory ban on all non-returnables since some markets may have characteristics, such as dispersed population and high tourism, which result in low trippage and will make the imposition of a returnable system socially as well as privately undesirable.

A high tax would raise the trippage of a returnable bottle since it increases the value of the returnable bottle to the beverage manufacturer; this will encourage him to improve the ease of returning bottles and will enable him to raise the deposit. Thus EPA, in their analysis of the effects of a 5 ¢ tax (US 3), assumed that the deposit on returnable bottles would be raised by 3 ¢.

This increase in trippage and the shift in market shares towards returnables will generate environmental benefits similar to those for a high mandatory deposit, namely, large reductions in litter, savings in solid waste management costs, decreased consumption of energy and materials and reduced water and air pollution. Again the only areas where gains are more than marginal are primarily in littering and, to a lesser extent, solid waste management.

The impacts of a 5 ¢ tax has been analysed by the EPA (US 3) and the resulting price change for beverage is shown in Table 5.8.

Table 5.8. % INCREASE IN PRICE DUE TO TAX*

BEVERAGE	RETURNABLE BOTTLE 15 TRIPS	NON-RETURNABLE BOTTLE	CAN
Beer	15	23.8	22
Soft Drinks	23	36	33

* The difference in the price change due to the tax for beer and soft drinks is due to the different total price of the two beverages.
SOURCE: US 3.

These price changes were expected to result in a decrease of 4% in beverage sales and a change to an all returnable system.

The loss of consumer convenience, due to the imposition of a high tax, is similar to that given for a high mandatory deposit (see Section 5.d). Consumers would be forced to pay an extra $ 1,613 million at 1969 prices to maintain convenience of not returning the containers. However, it is unlikely that this amount would be paid, rather consumers would be more likely to switch to a returnable system and return their bottles after use to reclaim their deposits.

Employment effects are expected to show a slight net gain. Losses would occur in the manufacturing industries, to be offset by larger gains in the production, distribution and retailing industries.

Investment write-offs are estimated at $ 1.4 billion and there would be an extra requirement for new investment of $ 1.2 billion.

The equity of the high tax system is not entirely satisfactory because consumers who buy beverages but do not litter them will still have to pay the tax. However, this may be considered more equitable than the present system whereby all members of society pay the price of littering whether they consume beverages or not, and the tax will have a direct impact on the litterbug to the extent that it results in a rise in the deposit on a returnable bottle, which the litterbug forfeits when he litters the bottle.

The high tax would be easier to administer than the regulatory policies (Sections 5.d and 5.e) because of its reliance on market forces and EPA (US 3) suggests that the existing taxation machinery could be used and the tax "should present no significant administrative problem".

One essential advantage of the high/medium tax is its flexibility. It could be set by each country at the level which yields the maximum surplus of environmental benefits over economic impact costs. Section 5.h will show that the low litter tax does not result in any major change in container market shares but merely halts the current trend away from returnables. Therefore the adverse economic impacts of the tax could be eased if it was gradually raised from a low litter tax to a medium/high reallocative tax according to a predetermined and definite phasing in schedule, which would enable the beverage industry to adjust their future plans in line with the new economic environment.

The only actual exemple of a high tax policy occurred in Norway in 1974. The tax was used primarily to remove the metal can from the beverage container market and successfully achieved this objective. The production of beer in cans was 12 million in 1973 (2.6% of total sales) and by 1975 it had been reduced to 1.4 million (0.3% of total beer sales). This was achieved with the imposition of a 30% tax on all non-returnable beverage containers. The importance of the Norwegian experience lies in the effectiveness of their tax policy. The costs were not very substantial due to the very small market share of cans at the time of the imposition of the tax and therefore this policy may be considered extremely useful in preventing a trend from becoming established. This is in complete contrast to the estimates summarized above of the impacts of such a policy for the USA where the non-returnables, particularly the can, are well established.

5.g. Product Charges for Solid Waste

In the discussion of the beverage container and solid waste (Section 4.b), it was shown that the present charging system for solid waste led to inefficiencies in most countries. Particularly noticeable is the lack of incentive to reduce solid waste by either the producer or the consumer. The product charge attempts to overcome this problem by pricing the cost of disposal at the point of manufacture. This will lead to two main results. Firstly, producers will have an incentive to reduce waste, improve recyclability or improve secondary material markets for materials relevant to their production process. This will occur because any product that does not enter the waste stream would be exempt from the product charge. Secondly, products which are solid waste intensive such as heavily packaged goods will become relatively more expensive than products which are not. This price adjustment will be a direct incentive for consumers to alter their purchasing decisions towards goods which are less likely to enter the waste stream.

It should be clearly understood that product charges are designed primarily to correct market mechanism deficiencies; the subsequent finance raised through the charges are of secondary importance. The main objective of this approach is 'to internalize" the external costs associated with solid waste collection and disposal.

The level at which the charge should be set may be determined by the cost of solid waste collection and disposal. Usually, weight is considered to be the easiest determinant of cost but it is possible, in those instances where volume is considered more relevant, to estimate costs on this basis. Weight is appropriate for most products and any alternative for specific products must be judged upon the extra administrative difficulties which are likely to be caused. Presently proposals in the USA include a 1.3 ¢ per pound charge ($ 26 per tonne) based on solid waste costs estimated for 1974. The only exception here is that non-flexible packaging would be charged on an item basis of 0.5 ¢ and this presumably is the proposed charge for beverage containers.

One of the difficulties of this approach is the consideration of which products should be charged. The USA proposal applies to all packaging products as this is clearly a large proportion of all municipal solid waste. Administratively, it would be more efficient to deal with packaging as a whole rather than product by product, because the entire subject could be dealt with in one bill rather than one bill per product. It is also feasible to consider large bulky items which require special collection and disposal costs under the charge proposals. The charge for these goods may be estimated more directly.

In order to operate an incentive for producers to reduce the quantity of material entering the solid waste stream it is necessary to exempt recycled products from the charge. This will give these products a clear price advantage over their virgin counterparts, which would in turn lead to a greater demand for secondary materials and stimulate recycling.

The revenue raised from product charges should ideally be redistributed to local municipalities because the costs of solid waste disposal are borne by them. Whether the funds are used for solid waste management or not may be decided at the local level; if they are, then the local municipality will have more funds available from which it can provide better services to the community; if not, then presumably local taxes or rates will be reduced. Whether this redistribution is feasible depends largely on the flexibility of the taxation system for each particular country.

The impacts of a product charge upon increased recycling are summarized in Table 5.9 for the USA (US 23).

The result of the charge will give a $ 17 per ton price advantage to recycled glass (cullet), which is equivalent to a 70% increase in value. This is anticipated to increase the availability of cullet by 8 to 15 times current levels. These impacts apply equally favourably to the other materials shown in Table 5.9.

Price increases are anticipated to be small due to the relatively low cost of solid waste handling (less than 1% of Gross Domestic Product, GDP). These price increases are offset to some extent by the benefits gained by the additional funds accruing to the municipalities. For beverages these price increases are for beer 2.2% and for soft drinks 4.1%. These price increases are substantially higher than the average because the 0.5 ¢ per rigid package is substantially higher than the more generally applicable $ 26 per tonne charge.

It is clear that the product charge policy has great potential for increased recycling if applied to all packaging products. The impacts

Table 5.9. REDUCTION IN CONSUMPTION OF PACKAGING
MATERIALS AS A RESULT OF PRODUCT CHARGES
(000's tonnes/year)

PACKAGING MATERIAL	WASTE REDUCTION EFFECTS	RESOURCE RECOVERY EFFECT	TOTAL
Paper	232	1,078	1,310
Plastics	40	0	40
Glass	216	4,078	4,294
Steel	238	2,532	2,770
Aluminium	8	244	252

SOURCE: US 23.

on beverage containers is likely to be equally substantial, with a greater usage of cullet in glass bottle production.

5.h. A Low Litter Tax on Beverage Containers

A low litter tax was implemented in the Washington State Litter Control Act of 1971. This Act imposed on manufacturers a tax of $ 150 per million dollars (i.e. .015%) of the sales values of packaging products "which are reasonably related to the litter problem". The revenue generated by the tax is used to finance educational and clean-up campaigns for litter reduction. EPA (US 3) has analyzed the effects expected from a national low litter tax of 0.5 ¢ on all beverage containers (returnable and non-returnable) the details of which are summarized below.

The tax would increase the price of beverages in non-returnables by about 2.3-3.5% while the price of beverages in returnables will remain virtually unchanged due to the amortization of the tax by trippage. However, the low size of the tax means that the increase in price differential in favour of returnables will not be sufficiently great to have much impact on container market shares or total beverage consumption, so that the low litter tax itself would result in small environmental benefits and economic impact costs on the beverage producers and consumers.

Sweden introduced, in 1973, a tax of 10 ore (2 ¢) on beverage containers and, although the purpose of the tax was to raise revenue to finance food subsidies, the committee on costs of environmental management analysed the economic and environmental effects of the tax. The committee found that the tax resulted in a rise in the deposit for 33 cl returnable bottles, from 15 ore to 25 ore (SWE 6), and a shift from non-returnable to returnable bottles whose market shares changed by 2-4 percentage points while the can's market share remained constant, as can be seen in Tables 2.4 and 2.5 in Section 2. This small change in market shares has resulted in a net increase in employment, which like other economic impacts was small, and marginal declines in solid waste and energy consumption of about 1/3% and 1/100% respectively (SWE 3, SWE 5). One possible failing of the above analysis is that it compares the pre with the post-legislative situation and hence does not take into account whether the tax led to a reversal of the trend away from returnables; but, even when this is considered, the effects of the tax would still not be great and the committee's conclusion that "the levy has not impacted materially on costs, employment and environment" is still valid.

The low litter tax is easy to administer through current taxation machinery and received popular support in Washington, but the essential benefit of the tax is the revenue it raises. EPA estimate that a 0.5 ¢ tax would raise $ 219 million in 1969 and $ 385 million in 1976, on the basis of projected trends in the beverage market (US 3), and SWE 3 estimates that a 5 ore increase in the duty would yield S Kr 50 million ($\simeq$ $ 11 million).

The Washington, but not the Swedish, legislation specifically allocated this revenue to pay for anti-litter education and clean-up measures such as increased litter collections, provision of receptacles and stricter enforcement of litter laws. A URS study (US 24) shows that there has been a 60% reduction in accumulated litter over the period 1971-75 which represents an annual reduction of 12-15% per annum, and further diminishing annual reductions were forecast so that by 1995 a 80% reduction would have been achieved. Section 4.c showed that litter was a major external cost of the beverage container, but that it was also the area where the data was the least secure on account of different methodologies used by the surveys and the effect on littering rates of important determining variables that are unconnected with the policy (e.g. weather, traffic levels). A more detailed analysis of the URS study would be necessary to establish whether an upward or downward revision of their estimates was required. Stern (US 17) analysed two area survey results from the Washington State Litter Survey claiming a 94% reduction in litter over the period May 1973 to September 1974 and found these results to be excessive. A closer examination of the data revealed reductions of 49% by volume and 53% by unit count. Stern showed that the volume litter reductions were the same in both Oregon and Washington, but that the unit count reductions were greater in Washington.

This Washington style approach represents the 'people problem' approach, where littering is felt to be determined by litterbugs and, therefore, should be cured by educational programs to create litter 'consciousness'. The benefits of this approach, over the Oregon style 'product problem' approach, are that it is a comprehensive attack on the whole spectrum of litter, while Oregon style action only tackles one section of litter, albeit an important one, and will only affect other litter to the extent the littering is encouraged by the presence of the conspicuous beverage container litter, as noted by AUS 1. Thus in Oregon there was a 12% increase in non-beverage related litter, but the 'people problem' Action Research Model (ARM) policy has produced 58-63% reductions in all litter in 3 American states (US 16).

There are, however, a number of problems to the 'people problem' ARM approach. The first is equity, since the costs of the expensive ARM programme are borne by all taxpayers, litterers and non-litterers alike. The Washington tax partially removes this problem since the tax burden is borne by the predominant component of litter - the beverage container, but it is still shared between the non-littering beverage consumers as well as the litterbugs. One way round this problem is to have structer enforcement of anti-litter laws and there has been a considerable boost in convictions in Washington since the law (US 24). However, EPA (US 3) and AUS 1 stress that litter laws are very costly and difficult to enforce due to the problems of catching and convicting offenders of what is an instantaneous action and they doubt whether the police force would be willing to divert stretched resources from more serious crimes.

The second problem relates to the long run effectiveness of the educational campaigns on littering behaviour, on which there is currently a lack of authoritative data. There is also need for research into the relative impacts on littering behaviour of the opposing forces of the educational campaigns on the one hand and the growing throwaway ethic generated by disposable products on the other. The above results from Washington suggest that the anti-litter campaigns do result in considerable reductions in litter, in the short run at least, but EPA quote survey results which show that the 21-35 year age group is the one that litters most (US 3) and this would have been the group most exposed to both the anti-litter education campaigns and the disposable ethic.

This raises the question of whether the costly anti-litter education and enforcement campaigns will have to be continually stepped up in order to prevent the growing underlying forces from leading to increase in litter. Consideration of these two problems prompts the reduction at source school, e.g. EPA (US 3) and AUS 1, to favour measures which attack the cause of the problem - the throwaway ethic -; they feel that anti-litter campaigns are a useful weapon to create a litter conscious, instead of a disposable, attitude in consumers but they doubt its effectiveness if used as the solitary weapon.

5.i. Standardization of Beverage Containers

Standardization of beverage containers would appear to be a possible methof for increasing the efficiency and feasibility of refillable container systems.

Unfortunately, no statistical data is available on this policy alternative, but the questions raised are discussed in a number of reports available to us (CAN 1, UK 23, US 14).

The advantages of standardization are usually considered to be the favourable effects upon the determinants of trippage - namely the willingness of retailers to supply refillable containers and the perceived loss of convenience suffered by consumers when returning containers. It is suggested that standardization will beneficially affect both determinants. Firstly, retailers will be more willing to stock standard bottles on a voluntary basis (since returned containers would require less sorting) which would increase the proportion of the refillable containers market share. Secondly, standardization would make it easier for consumers to return refillables by increasing the number of retailers where they can be returned and this would increase the average propensity to return refillable containers. It is also possible that costs may be reduced because containers would not necessarily need to be returned to the original packers and therefore transportation distances may be reduced.

One of the greatest problems facing the refillable container system has been found to be the difficulty of getting the consumers to return their used containers and any innovation that is likely to change consumers behaviour in this respect must not be overlooked.

Some indication of the possible impacts of standardization may be gleaned from those countries where standard bottles are predominantly in use.

In Ontario, the brewing industry uses a standard beer bottle and this is perceived to be a significant element in the effectiveness of that distribution system. In Oregon, the beverage container legislation includes an incentive system for standardization. If a refillable bottle is used by two or more beverage manufacturers, it may be certified by the Oregon Liquor Control Commission and is then subject to a lower minimum refundable deposit (i.e. 2 ¢ instead of 5 ¢). This will induce bottlers to retrieve used bottles because the cost of a returned bottle is now substantially cheaper than a newly produced one. The brewing industry has adopted this system and 'certified' beer bottles are predominantly in evidence in Oregon. The soft drinks producers have not, however, adopted this system and it is important to note that the return rate for beer bottles with a 2 ¢ deposit is greater than the return rate for soft drink bottles with a 5 ¢ deposit. This again points out the importance of retailer acceptance and customer convenience as more critical determinants of return rates than the size of the deposit.

In Norway, the beverage container system for beer and soft drinks is based upon compulsory standardization of bottles as to container size (35, 70 and 100 cl) and voluntary standardization as to colour, shape and weight. As a result of a voluntary agreement between the breweries bottles have to a very great extent been standardized. In 1975, 84% of all beer sold in Norway (97% of beer sold in containers) was marketed in standardized 35 and 70 cl bottles. A similar standardization has taken place for soft drink bottles. Particular brands of beer are sold in returnable bottles differing in shape and colour from the Norwegian standard bottles, but they have a very modest share of the market (2.1% in 1975). Nevertheless, as many as 14-15 different types of returnable bottles for beer and soft drinks are marketed in Norway.

All but a negligeable share of the retail market for beer and soft drinks in Norway is held by products sold in returnable bottles. The return rate of bottles for beer and soft drinks in Norway is at present around 99%. The trippage is estimated to an average of 35. These highly satisfactory results are mainly believed to be attributable to:
- the directives on container size;
- the voluntary agreement on standardization of bottles as to shape and colour;
- the relatively high, uniform deposit rates;
- the use of returnable crates.

It is, in the opinion of the Norwegian Government, considered that the advantages of standardizing beverage containers (high trippage, reduced littering, reduced solid waste, reduced production and distribution costs, customer convenience, etc.) far outweigh the disadvantages (possible inflexibility and marketing inconvenience), and that standardization of beverage containers is a key factor for obtaining a high return rate.

In Denmark, similarly satisfactory results emerge where a standard beer bottle is used by the brewers through voluntary cooperation. Trippage figures are estimated at 30-35, and it is considered that standard bottles are an important determinant of this high figure. Furthermore, a standard bottle allows a standard outer package which in Denmark achieves extremely high return rates; generally this outer packaging takes the form of a 24 or 30 bottle crate. It is interesting to note that there has been a change of shape of the standard beer bottle, which did not cause any marked dislocation (an inflexibility usually associated with standardization) because it was gradually phased in. Indeed, so long as the height, base diameter and top diameter of a bottle remain constant a great deal of variability is acceptable.

The problems of standardization are related to the inflexibility and marketing disadvantages associated with it.

A standard bottle used throughout an industry is likely to cause a disincentive to producers to develop new technology and decrease the costs of bottle manufacture. Improvements and cost-saving innovations would become difficult to adopt as it may necessitate throwing out the present stock of standard containers.

Much of the effectiveness of the one way container and its growth in the beverage container market is due to its adaptability as a marketing device. Shape, colour and size may be adjusted in order to differentiate the product and increase sales volume; standardization of the bottle would limit this flexibility and is therefore likely to the opposed by industry on these grounds, although the industry would still be able to use differences in the design of labels as a marketing device.

Clearly, in those countries were standardized bottles are well established the returnable bottle system becomes very efficient. The increased convenience to consumers and producers alike leads to high sustainable trippage rates which are fundamental for a returnable system. On these grounds, the standardization of beverage container systems would appear to be an extremely useful government policy.

5.i.1. Standardization and International Trade

No data is available from which the impacts of standardization on international trade may be assessed. However, it is clear that if one country adopts a standard bottle for a particular market, this will create a non-tariff trade barrier that will reduce the level of trade. Unless the standards are applied to all countries it must be expected that standardization will reduce trade. Where, however, two countries have the same standards the possibility of increasing the refillable container market share is greatly enhanced. As was stated above, one of the advantages of a standard bottle was the possible reduction in transport costs because the container does not have to be returned to the original packer. Since the cost of return is crucial to the commercial acceptability of a refillable system, it can be expected that the refillable system would be more economic where standardization between importer and exporter exists.

The extent to which trade in beer packed in containers is carried out is shown in Table 5.10.

Documentation of other types of beverages is less complete; the data available is given in Tables 5.11 and 5.12.

Unfortunately, the data for soft drinks and wine broken down into packaged and bulk imports and exports is not available; consequently it is not possible to show the actual size of the problem with respect to beverage containers alone. Obviously, only imports and exports packaged in ready to sell containers would be affected by beverage container legislation. It is understood that, particularly in the case of wine, a large proportion of trade is carried out in bulk containers and bottled by the importers of the various recipient countries.

This data yields the tentative conclusion that the level of international trade in <u>beverage containers</u> is small relative to production or

Table 5.10. IMPORTS AND EXPORTS OF BEER IN CONTAINERS 1975 (000's hl)

	IMPORTS	%[1]	EXPORTS	%[1]
Belgium/Luxembourg	189	1.3	834	6.13
Denmark	19	0.29	1,322	20.15
Finland	10	0.38	31	11.7
France	1,019	4.28	527	2.2
Germany	578	0.63	1,775	1.93
Italy	544	7.49	13	0.18
Netherlands	131	1.2	1,742	16.17
Norway	7	0.38	122	6.6
Sweden	397	8.2	18	0.38
Switzerland	187	4.1	11	0.24
U.K.	-	-	462	0.7

1. Imports/Exports as a percentage of total consumption.
SOURCE: EEC 3.

Table 5.11. TOTAL IMPORTS AND EXPORTS OF SOFT DRINKS (BULK AND PACKAGED) (000's hl) 1975

	IMPORTS	%[1]	EXPORTS	%[1]
Norway		0.35		
Switzerland	1.9 [2]	4.1		
Italy	303	2.28	180	1.36

1. Imports/Exports as a percentage of domestic production.
2. Imported in beverage containers.
SOURCE: EEC 4, correspondence with delegations.

Table 5.12.   EXPORTS OF WINE: 1975
(000's hl)

	EXPORTS	% OF PRODUCTION
Italy	14,125	20
France	5,935	9

SOURCE: EEC 4.

consumption. However, further documentation would be useful to substantiate this point over a wider spectrum of countries and beverages.

5.j. Recycling and Resource Recovery

Recycling is the name given to a processus which prevents used and unwanted products (in the consumers eyes) from entering the environment as waste, and returns them back into the production sector. It is important to make the conceptual distinction between recycling in the form of the re-use of a container for the same purpose as its previous use, and the more general meaning of recycling where the container is reduced to its basic constituents ready for remanufacture into either its original use (another container) or some other use. The previous policy measures considered (Sections 5.c-5.i) have been concerned with stimulating the former aspect, re-use, through actions to encourage the returnable bottle, but an alternative policy option open to the government, is to allow the market shares between returnable and non-returnable containers to be determined by market forces in an unrestrained manner and to concentrate on recycling, in the latter sense, as the means of solving the resource and solid waste management problems caused by the beverage container.

This policy option has been advocated (US 31, US 16, UK 4) on the grounds that it will reduce the adverse environmental impact of beverage containers and, since the policy does not entail any direct government intervention in the beverage market, it will not cause economic dislocation in the beverage industry.

5.j.1. Environmental Benefits of Recycling

Increased recycling, through source separation or resource recovery programmes, will reduce the volume of <u>solid waste</u> that has to be disposed. The benefit of this recycling approach, over the re-use approach of favouring the returnable bottle, is that it tackles all the recoverable materials in the solid waste stream and not just the beverage containers' share of these materials. Table 5.13 shows American estimates (US 32) of the practical maximum impact of increased recycling on solid waste.

Table 5.13 shows that if the recycling of the principal beverage container materials, glass and metal, could be increased so that a further 50% and 20%, respectively, of these materials in the solid waste stream was recycled then this would result in a 8.4% reduction in the weight of solid waste that has to be disposed. The Swiss glass collection schemes have resulted in a 6-10% reduction in household solid waste, and the experiments in Sweden for the separate collection of paper, glass and metal cans resulted in a 15-17% reduction in solid waste (SWE 7). These two recycling schemes are considered in more detail in Section 5.j.3.

However, care needs to be taken in converting these reductions in solid waste into monetary savings. First the collection of municipal solid waste accounts for the great proportion, 75%, of solid waste management costs and recycling may have no impact on the total quantity of solid waste to be collected. Thus resource recovery programmes still require the collection of all municipal solid waste for delivery to the treatment plants, and the separate collection of selected materials (e.g. paper etc.) entails an extra and possibly more expensive collection process. Second the fixed cost element of disposal and collection costs will mean that, in the short run at least, variations in the quantities of solid waste may not result in similar costs savings. This is especially true for the collection of municipal solid waste which may be a statutory obligation, and the sensitivity of disposal costs to changes in the quantities of solid waste will depend upon each municipality's particular circumstances (e.g. current disposal methods and availability of landfill sites).

Table 5.14 shows that, if the recycling of metal cans was increased, then the solid waste generated by the metal can was reduced by 18% so that now the metal can generates less solid waste than the 10 trip returnable soft drink bottle. A return rate of 18.4% for metal cans is the rate achieved in Ontario where there is a deposit of 15 ¢ per dozen cans.

Recycling may reduce the pollution generated by the beverage container systems in two ways. First the addition of recycled glass (cullet) reduces the temperature required for melting in the glass manufacturing process and this reduces the particulate emissions. Second the recycled beverage containers will replace virgin raw materials and hence save the pollution generated by virgin raw material extraction and processing. However, these pollution savings have to be offset against the pollution from recycling, principally from the transportation and collection of the waste materials. The EPA (US 32) says that the use of recycled materials generally causes less pollution than the use of virgin materials and (US 6) shows that the recycling of aluminium cans reduces the pollution generated by the manufacture of aluminium cans.

Table 5.13. ESTIMATES OF PRACTICAL MAXIMUM IMPACT OF INCREASED RECYCLING ON MUNICIPAL SOLID WASTE FOR THE USA

MATERIAL	WEIGHT (DRY) IN SOLID WASTE IN 1968 (10^6 tons)	ASSUMED POSSIBLE INCREASE IN RECYCLING — INCREASE IN % OF MATERIAL IN WASTE THAT IS RECYCLED	ASSUMED POSSIBLE INCREASE IN RECYCLING — WEIGHT (10^6 tons)	% REDUCTION IN TOTAL SOLID WASTE RESULTING FROM INCREASED RECYCLING
Paper and Board	40	15	6.0	6.0
Metal	12	20	2.4	2.4
Glass	12	50	6.0	6.0
Rubber Tyres	2	80	1.6	1.6
Other	34	0	0	0
Total	100		16.0	16.0

NOTE: The increase in recycling rates shown in this table, reflects EPA assumptions merely to illustrate effects on solid waste. They do not necessarily reflect the technical limits to recycling.

SOURCE: US 32.

Table 5.14. THE IMPACT OF THE INCREASED RECYCLING OF METAL CANS ON THE SOLID WASTE GENERATION - COMPARISONS OF THE RETURNABLE BOTTLE AND METAL CAN FOR 240,000 FLUID OUNCES OF BEVERAGE

BEVERAGE	CONTAINER	WEIGHT (lbs) IN SOLID WASTE OF PRIMARY CONTAINERS ONLY	COMPARISON RATIO
Soft Drink ..	10 oz. Returnable Bottle (10 trip)	2,100	1.00 : 1
Beer	12 oz. Returnable Bottle (21.5 trip)	494	0.24 : 1
Beer	12 oz. Metal Can - Return rate for recycling = 0%	2,247	1.07 : 1
Beer	12 oz. Metal Can - Return rate for recycling = 18.4%	1,836	0.87 : 1

SOURCE CAN 1.

The manufacture of containers out of recycled materials, instead of virgin raw materials, may result in a considerable saving in the energy requirements of the beverage container systems, as can be seen in Table 5.15.

Table 5.15. % CHANGE IN TOTAL SYSTEMS ENERGY REQUIREMENTS WHEN 100% RECYCLED MATERIAL IS USED INSTEAD OF VIRGIN RAW MATERIAL

CONTAINER SYSTEM	% CHANGE
Aluminium Can	-78%
Plastic (ABS) Bottle	-62%
All Steel Can	-39%
Non-Returnable Bottle	+23%

SOURCE: US 6.

These savings are greatest for the aluminium can and plastic bottle on account of the energy intensive virgin raw material processes, which are by-passed when recycled material is used. There is some controversy over the effect of glass recycling on the total energy requirements. The addition of cullet to the furnace results in a 12-22% reduction in the energy requirements of glass container manufacturing (US 2) and the cullet will replace virgin raw materials (e.g. soda ash) and hence the energy required for their processing; but these energy savings have to be offset against the energy requirements of the collection and separation processes. Hannon (US 8) produces data which show that these collection and separation requirements outweigh the savings so that the use of recycled glass, instead of virgin raw material, raises the energy requirement of the glass bottle systems. However, RTI (US 2) shows that the use of 100% recycled glass cullet would reduce the energy requirements of the non-returnable bottle systems by 11%, and other studies (SWI 4, SWI 6, UK 31) give further evidence to support this view. The discrepancy between the two views results from the different assumptions used for the type of the collection and separation process. One assumption (US 6, US 8) is that the relatively energy intensive wet separation process is used. However separation techniques, currently being developed and operated in many countries, use considerably less energy.

In conclusion, therefore, increased recycling will reduce the energy requirements, the solid waste and the pollution generated by the beverage containers. Fig. 5.1 shows that at high recycling rates the aluminium can and plastic bottle systems require less energy than the 5-trip returnable bottle and thus increased recycling will help to reduce the unfavourable position of the non-returnable containers with respect to these environmental impact categories. However, Section 4 found that a central area of concern over the beverage container issue was litter, since this was one of the areas where the beverage containers' impact was most significant. Although a slight reduction in litter may result from schemes to encourage consumers to return containers to recycling depots or collection bins, recycling will not offset the adverse impact of the non-returnables on litter.

5.j.2. Practical recycling possibilities

So far the analysis has only considered the environmental gains from hypothetical recycling rates. Thus Table 5.13 and 5.15 show the potential energy and solid waste savings that would result from certain recycling rates which were chosen for exposition purposes and not to reflect the current recycling situation. Thus the 100% recycling rate of beverage containers shown in Table 5.15 could not be obtained on account of handling and melt losses in the remanufacturing process. The RTI (US 2) estimates these losses to amount to 13% for the steel and aluminium cans and 8% for the glass bottle so that even

Figure 5.1
THE TOTAL ENERGY REQUIREMENTS OF ALTERNATIVE BEVERAGE CONTAINER SYSTEMS
WITH RESPECTS TO DIFFERENT LEVELS OF RECYCLING

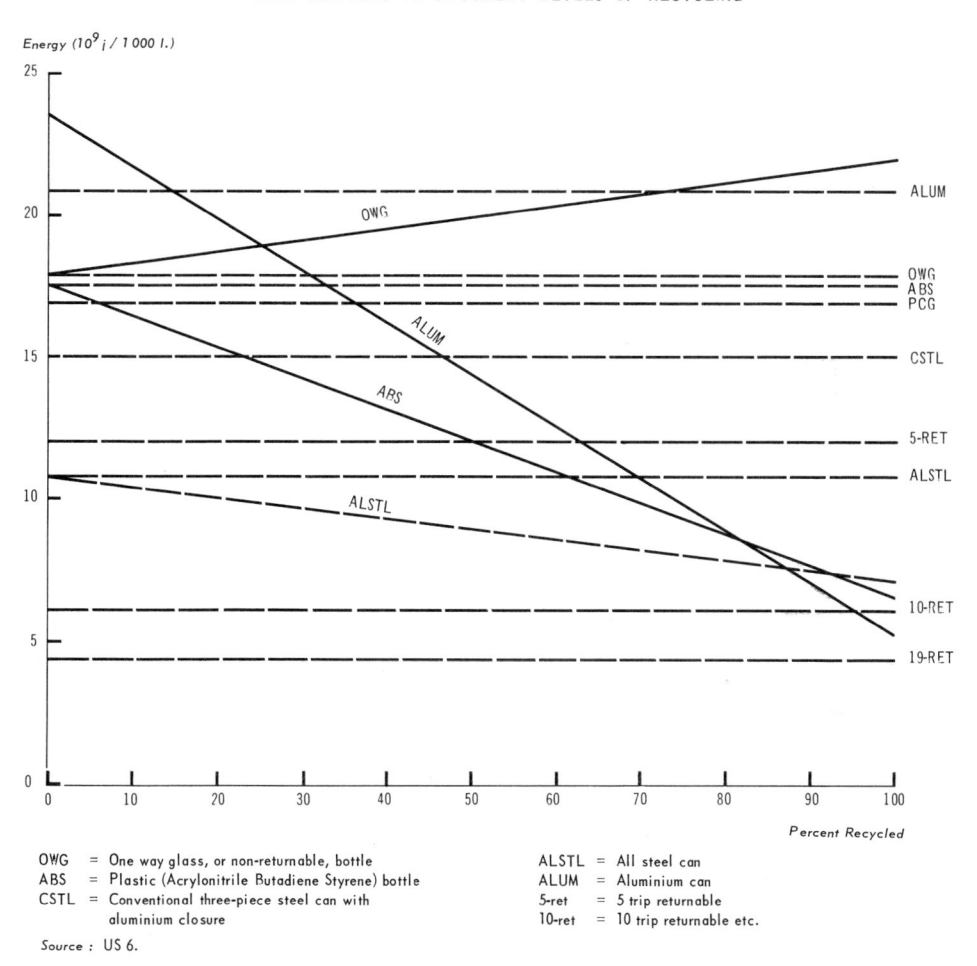

Energy (10^9 j / 1 000 l.)

Percent Recycled

OWG	= One way glass, or non-returnable, bottle	ALSTL	= All steel can
ABS	= Plastic (Acrylonitrile Butadiene Styrene) bottle	ALUM	= Aluminium can
CSTL	= Conventional three-piece steel can with aluminium closure	5-ret	= 5 trip returnable
		10-ret	= 10 trip returnable etc.

Source : US 6.

if 100% of the beverage containers could be collected, then this would only equal yields of recovered materials of 87% for the metal cans and 91% for the glass bottles.

It is necessary to consider the problems involved in recycling each container material in order to determine what recycling rates are currently attainable now and in the future, and therefore the size of the potential environmental impact savings that recycling can be expected to generate.

Table 5.16. % RECOVERY AND RECYCLING RATES OF BEVERAGE CONTAINERS

CONTAINER MATERIAL	1975	1985 (FORECAST)
Glass containers		
- recovery rate	2.3	4.0
- net recycling at 91%	2.1	3.6
Steel Cans		
- recovery rate	1.9	12.5
- net recycling at 87%	1.7	10.8
Aluminium Cans		
- recovery rate [1]	24.2	45.0
- net recycling at 87%	21.0	39.0

1. This is the percentage recovery of all aluminium cans and not of the total aluminium used in beverage cans since it excludes aluminium tabs and ends on steel cans. If the recovery rate was calculated on the basis of all aluminium used in beverage cans, it would drop by about one-third e.g. the 1975 figure would be 17% instead of 24.2%.
SOURCE: US 2.

Table 5.16, shows American estimates of current and future recycling rates for beverage containers and these figures suggest that there are certain problems involved in the collection, separation and marketing of the various materials that limit the extent to which recycling can reduce the adverse environmental impact of the non-returnable beverage containers.

The only material for which high recycling rates are forecast is aluminium. In those countries where aluminium is used extensively (e.g. USA), aluminium cans are fairly easily converted into new can metal and the high value of the scrap metal makes it worthwhile for the aluminium companies and some packers (e.g. Coors) to set up collection centres which pay 0.75 ₡ for each can returned and are said to experience return rates of 50%, although these return rates have been questioned (US 33) on the grounds that the aluminium returned to Coors' collection centres contain other aluminium products (e.g. foil, trays, etc.) and cans from other companies. Therefore, these return rates are not representative of the national situation. Also the RTI data in Table 5.13 has been criticised for using excessively optimistic forecasts for the development of resource recovery programmes and for overstating the expected increase in the aluminium can market share of the beverage market. It has been suggested (NETH 6, UK 22) that, in Europe, the level of aluminium can recycling is lower than the steel can recycling rate since the aluminium can is a comparative rarety.

Tin cans are relatively easy to recover from solid waste, e.g. through magnetic separation, but can be difficult to recycle on account of the presnnce of impurities and contaminants such as the tin coating, lead soldering and possibly an aluminium top as well. In some countries (e.g. UK) there is a ready market for recovered tin cans in steel founding where this can content can be metallurgically beneficial (UK 7). However, the degradation of the tin cans during use prevents their utilisation in the manufacture of new cans and the impureties in tin plate scrap, especially the tin, are regarded as undesirable tramp elements in other steel making processes, since they can cause refractory damage to the furnace and impair the quality of the final product. This means that tin plate scrap is regarded as low grade scrap for which there is a low demand in some countries, and the low scrap value can render the recycling process uneconomic.

De-tinning by electrolysis produces a higher grade steel scrap for which there is greater demand, and also recovers a valuable material, tin. However, the de-tinning process is adversely affected by the presence of contaminants, such as lead, and the aluminium top requires an additional separation process which EPA (US 32) estimates to cost an extra $ 10-15 per ton, although it has been suggested (NETH 6) that development is currently underway to remove the aluminium top. Fornerod (NETH 7) shows that the detinning of tinplate scrap raises the value of the scrap steel from H. fl. 100 to H. fl. 175 per ton and recovers about 2.5 kg of tin (with a value of about H. fl. 45) per ton of tin cans. However, the de-tinning process costs about H. fl. 130 per ton so that, at present there appears to be a limited potential for de-tinning to raise the recycling rate of tin cans. The considerable reduction in the thickness of the tin coating and the relatively static price of tin in the 1950's and 60's led to a decline in the quantity of post consumer can waste which has been de-tinned. The steep increase in the price of tin has caused a re-awakening of interest in recent years.

In the UK, Metal Box Co., Batchelor Robinson and the British Steel Corporation undertook a joint study of tinplate recycling (UK 2) which showed it to be technically feasible but not so far economically viable.

Unlike recycled tinplate, waste glass or cullet can be used to manufacture new containers and in fact the addition of cullet is beneficial to the glass manufacturing process since the cullet reduces the temperature required in the melting process. Experimental tests undertaken in the Netherlands indicate that, in theory, 70% mixed unsorted cullet can be used in the production of green glass containers without any problem (NETH 5). Thus there is no shortage of demand for the right sort of cullet. However, foreign post-consumer cullet can contain contaminants, such as coloured glass and metallic rings, which are detrimental to the production process, especially for clear glass. The problem of glass recycling centres round the difficulty of providing at a reasonable cost, a continuous supply of 'clean' foreign cullet which satisfies the glass manufactures' cullet specification limits. These limits become increasingly tighter as the percentage of cullet used increases.

One potential source of such 'clean' foreign cullet is the returnable bottles that are broken at the bottler during the refilling stage. This comprises a major portion of the cullet used in some countries (e.g. Denmark) since it represents a fairly homogenous source which should be of known composition and should contain few contaminants. Swiss data (SWI 4) suggests that this source accounts for 30,000 tonnes of waste cullet each year, and a system operates in the UK where the broken returnable bottles are stored in 'pugbins'. These 'pugbins' are formed from the pallets, on which new bottles are delivered, and the full 'pugbins' are returned on the same lorry that delivers the new bottles. This saves transport costs which can be an important factor preventing the collection of post-consumer waste glass by communities far from a glass works.

At present there is very litte recycling of plastic containers. This is basically due to the contamination of the plastic polymer by other plastics and by other components in household waste, which presents a difficult and expensive separation problem. Energy recovery probably represents the most promising area for the recycling of plastics, which have a high calorific value.

5.j.3. Source Separation of Recyclable Materials by Households

There are three possible approaches that Member countries can use to ease the separation and collection problems of recycling beverage container materials. These are source separation by the households with either the municipality collecting the separated materials or the consumers taking the containers to central collection points, or mechanical separation of mixed domestic refuse in resource recovery plants.

Experiments with the separate collection of specific materials have been undertaken in a number of countries and have met with varying degrees of success.

In Canada a pilot study was undertaken in the township of Burlington (CAN 3) for the seaprate collection of newspaper, metal cans and glass which showed that the quantities of these materials collected represented 72 %, 44% and 55 %, respectively, of the total quantities available in household waste. This yielded a revenue of $ 34 per week but the costs of the scheme amounted to about $ 160 per week so that it was decided not to extend the scheme, especially since this would involve increased costs of transporting the extra recycled materials to markets further afield. Also the study found that the participation in the scheme was significantly lower than had been forecast by questionnaire surveys and that the first collection of materials contained significant quantities of contaminants (e.g. metal rings, mixing of clear and coloured glass). This made them unsuitable for recycling, although this problem was solved by a further issue of instructions for separation.

In the UK, Redfearn National Glass Ltd. investigated the viability of the separate collection of glass for the city of York. This scheme collected about 11 tons of glass which represented about 30% of the total glass in household waste and yielded a total revenue of £ 71. However, the high collection costs, £ 35 per ton, meant that the scheme yielded a deficit of nearly £ 30 per ton of glass collected; this led Redfearn National Glass to conclude that separate collection was only likely to be viable if other recyclable materials (e.g. metal, newspaper) were collected as well as glass (UK 5).

During the preparation of this report, the UK Oxfam 'wastesaver' scheme in Huddersfield has been visited and from this experience useful informations was obtained on source separation. Originally the 'wastesaver' operation centred on the provision of a 'dumpy' to about 5,000 households in the Huddersfield area. This dumpy contained four coloured sacks, one for newspaper, one for mixed waste paper, one for glass, plastics and tin cans and a sack for bric-a-bric (rags, books, etc.). The psychological impact of saving waste to enable Oxfam to help the Third World has played a large part in the good public response to the scheme, which yields about 7-8 lbs per week of separated materials from participating households. This is 26% of the average 28 lbs of waste normally generated by households each week. Nevertheless the dumpies frequently contain much worthless junk (e.g. old boots) and contaminants (e.g. aluminium tops of bottles) which make hand sorting of the waste glass necessary. Furthermore the dumpy collection system has been hit by rising transport and labour costs so that former plans to expand the dumpies are unlikely to be realized.

Table 5.17 shows the cost of transporting and processing the recycled materials in comparison with the final prices received. However, it must be mentioned that Table 5.17 shows the full economic costs of these operations, it does not represent the cost actually

Table 5.17. COMPARISON OF THE TRANSPORT, PROCESSING AND SALE PRICE PER HOME FOR EACH OF THE RECYCLED MATERIALS (AUGUST 1976)

	COSTS £ PER HOME		SALE PRICE £ PER HOME
	TRANSPORT	PROCESSING	
Paper	25	21	24
Glass	24	23	10
Tin	24	53	35

NOTE: The transport costs relate to each materials share of the dumpy collection costs. Other collection methods are also used (e.g. from trade sources) which have slightly lower transport costs.
SOURCE: UK 33.

incurred by Oxfam. These are lower on account of the considerable financial assistance that Oxfam wastewater has received (e.g. from government and industrial bodies). Also the figures relate to August 1976, only 12 months after the project was started. Since then improvements have been made and the throughout of recycled material increased so that by February 1977, sales revenue had increased by 17% while costs had been reduced by 14%. Nevertheless, in February 1977, the operation was still loosing £ 1,100 per month so that a reappraisal was undertaken which resulted in a substantial reorganisation of the scheme in an attempt to make it profitable. This reorganisation is currently underway and the principal element of interest is the replacement of the four sack dumpy by a one sack dumpy containing only waste paper and textiles. The collection of tin, glass, and plastic has been discontinued. No markets could be found for the mixed plastic waste and the prices received for the waste glass and tinplate were not even covering their direct processing costs, let alone enabling a contribution to be made towards transport costs and overheads. This highlights the costly problem involved in the collection and processing of waste materials which frequently makes their recycling not viable, even for an organisation like Oxfam which has benefitted from a favourable response from households volunteers and workers, government and the industries concerned.

Sweden seems to be one country which has experienced success with separate collection schemes. The Swedish experiment, undertaken by the Swedish Institute for Resource Recovery (SWE 7), required the householder to separate paper into one bag and glass along with metal into another bag; this glass/metal mixture was then processed in a

PLM 'Frans' plant into cullet, tinplate and aluminium. The purpose of the study was to discover whether households would be willing to participate in this separation procedure. A participation rate of 70% was achieved which, it was felt, might possibly be increased to 80%. The participation rate was found to be higher in family townhouses than appartments on account of the greater storage space available and the higher consumption levels in these areas. Also for these townhouses, Sweden operates a system of solid waste charges that vary with the level of the solid waste generated by the households. This means that these householders, participating in the separation scheme, benefit directly from reduced charges for the collection of their remaining solid waste. The Swedish Institute for Resource Recovery estimates that the recycled materials could be sold for about S KR 90 per tonne while the extra collection costs amounted to S KR 120 per tonne so that the scheme produced a deficit of S KR 30 per tonne. However, the scheme resulted in a 17% reduction in the level of solid waste generated. If, in the long run at least, this results in a reduction in solid waste collection and disposal costs of 4.25% and 17% respectively, then the study shows that the separation scheme would yield a net reduction in solid waste management costs of between 3-7% depending upon whether landfill or incineration is the disposal method used.

The particular circumstances of the local municipalities will determine whether any short or long term savings in collection and disposal costs are attainable. Therefore the viability of separate collection schemes depends upon the success of the information campaign to encourage householders to separate materials in the right manner (i.e. free from contaminants) so that the revenue raised and the above savings are sufficient to offset the extra collection costs.

Considerable investigation of recycling has been undertaken in the Netherlands (NETH 7, NETH 5) which suggests that these extra collection costs are so great that, even when one takes into account the social benefits of recycling, the separate collection schemes may well not be socially viable. Therefore it is suggested that collection costs should be reduced by encouraging the consumers to transport the waste materials to strategically sited collection bins or recycling centres and such schemes are currently in operation in the USA, Netherlands, Switzerland, Denmark and Germany. However, although this hidden subsidy from the public results in savings in solid waste management costs for the municipality, it does not necessarily result in savings in resources. Thus EPA (US 6) show that, if one considers the energy required for the consumers to transport the container, then the energy savings from using 100% recycled, instead of virgin, aluminium are reduced from the 78% figure shown in Table 5.15 to 59%.

In America, recycling centres operate for the collection of various materials, the most notable of these are the aluminium collection centres run by Coors Company. As mentioned earlier, these centres pay .75 ¢ for each aluminium can returned. However, the low scrap value of the other materials (glass and tinplate) means that it is not possible to offer similar bounties for these materials and the return of these materials has to rely upon the goodwill and environmental consciousness of the consumer. The low density and bulkiness of tinplate cans results in the filled collection bins containing an insufficient weight or recycled material to make this type of collection process appropriate for metal cans, since the revenue from the recycled metal does not usually cover the costs of procuring it. However, the results of the Dutch, Danish, Swiss and German schemes suggest that this type of collection procedure may be viable for the heavier and more dense glass containers.

In the Netherlands, a study (NETH 5) was undertaken of a collection scheme based on the following lines. Consumers take non-returnable glass bottles to collection bins situated in residential and shopping areas. The contents of the bins are then taken to a storage depot and then on to a cullet merchant who sorts and crushes the cullet. This sorting is necessary on account of the presence of excessive contaminants (e.g. metal sealings) and the crushing process reduces the volume of cullet and hence final transport costs to the glass works. The study found that the mixed cullet could be sold for H fl. 45 per tonne which compared with costs of H fl. 35-40 per tonne for the crushing and sorting operations and the transport of the cullet from the depots to the cullet merchant and then into the glass works. This left H fl. 10 to cover the costs of collecting the cullet from the bins and for the costs related to the collection bins; such costs included the rent of the bin site, depreciation costs of the bins and the costs of cleaning and supervising the collection bins. This was necessary on account of the problems of vandalism and the mess made at the sites. In many circumstances these costs far exceeded the H fl. 5-H fl. 10 per tonne margin. However, it was felt that supermarkets should bear the costs of supervision and cleaning of the sites in the shopping areas, on the grounds that it is the supermarkets that benefit from non-returnable containers. The same study (NETH 5) also suggested that further cost savings could be obtained by rationalizing the system of collecting from the bins. One possible alternative would be to use a 'dump master' which would collect the cullet from a number of the bins and transport it straight to the cullet merchant. This would save storage costs and could be made economically sound but only in metropolitan areas covering more than 1 1/4 million people.

In Switzerland an extensive system of collection points is covering about 60% of the total population. In 1976 this scheme generated about 63,000 tonnes of cullet, which represents about 25% of household waste glass (SWI 5).

In one town in Denmark (Birkerod) a total of 250 tons of glass containers were deposited in central collection bins; this represents about 50% of glass used by households and the collected glass was separated into refillable containers, which were sold to bottle merchants, and non-refillable containers, which are recycled as cullet. At present this system incurs a slight deficit but another town has introduced a modified version which is hoped to break even.

In Germany a successfull glass separation programme operates which, in 1976, yielded a total of 260,000 tonnes of cullet. This programme embodies the provision at strategic points of collection bins and the use of a dumpmaster type system to collect the cullet from the bins. These operations are profitably run by private contractors who do not receive any subsidy from public funds although some local authorities forgo the payment of rent on the collection bin sites. The very good public response has played a large part in the success of these recycling schemes. Currently 4-15 kg of waste glass per inhabitant are collected annually which represents 10-37% of the total glass normally in the solid waste stream. In some areas three separate containers are provided. One for clear flint glass, one for amber and one for green glass. This colour separation process raises the marketing potential for the cullet and has been satisfactorily undertaken by the public who also help with the cleaning and supervision of the bin sites. The quality of cullet received is generally of a fairly good standard although the presence of contaminants has in some instances resulted in the rejection of a cullet batch; this has prompted the private contractors and glass manufactures to increasingly install cullet cleaning equipment. The good response of the German public can be largely attributed to the good advertising campaign and the system of charging for solid waste that is operated in many parts of Germany. Under this system the German householder has to pay extra for additional solid waste that he generates; this is likely to create and environmental awareness of the problems of solid waste and creates a direct financial incentive for the households to participate in the recycling campaign. It is significant to note that the two countries that operate successful household recycling campaigns, Sweden and Germany, are those that operate this direct system of charging for solid waste.

5.j.4. <u>Resource Recovery Schemes with mechanical separation</u>

Resource recovery from post-consumer solid waste is rapidly becoming an attractive area of research in many countries. The potential for resource recovery is very largely due to the quantity of waste material that is presently being discarded by consumers. The object of resource recovery is to provide a reliable system for waste disposal while at the same time affording as much protection to the environment as possible. Resource recovery from refuse has the advantage over other recycling techniques in that the refuse is treated in its conglomerate form, and therefore costly pre-separation techniques are not required. This also alleviates the problems arising from the need for consumer cooperation which is frequently crucial to other recycling systems. It is largely because of this independence that the reliability of this approach can be achieved.

One of the most well documented resource recovery schemes is operated by the Bureau of Mines in Maryland University. This pilot plant operates with a throughput of 5 tons per day. Separation is achieved through an involved system of air classifiers, magnets, shredders and screens. The exact method of operation is too detailed to relate here (see US 35) but the results that have been achieved with this equipment are of interest. A typical breakdown of the end products from this process is given in Table 5.18.

Table 5.18. TYPICAL PILOT PRODUCTS OBTAINED FROM RAW REFUSE

PRODUCT	%
Light combustibles (fuel)	59.3
Ferrous metal	7.6
Aluminium	0.8
Heavy non-ferrous metal	0.2
Glass	10.5
Heavy combustibles (fuel)	5.0
Putrescibles dewatered to 50% solids (fuel)	6.6
Fine glass, grit dirt and ceramics	10.0

SOURCE: US 35.

This table shows the potential for resource recovery; only the last item (fine glass, grit, etc.) is of no value. What is interesting to note is that the majority of the refuse (70.9%) may be used as a fuel. It should also be noted that although these figures are as reliable as possible there is a great deal of variance in the mixture contained in post-consumer solid waste. This variability may be due to a number of factors including season, location, and the level of industrialisation.

On the basis of experiments with this pilot plant the saving and revenues for full scale plants have been estimated for daily throughputs of 500 and 1,000 tons of refuse per day. These are shown in Table 5.19.

Clearly, these savings are private benefits and it is likely that the social benefits may be larger because no account is taken of conservation of valuable materials and energy resources. Savings will also accrue because this system for disposal will avoid pollution of air, water and land frequently associated with waste disposal operations.

However, what is not considered in this analysis is the part which the beverage container plays in this system. From Table 5.18 it is shown that metal and glass account for some 19.1% of all refuse, and thus this figure represents a maximum for the beverage container

Table 5.19. SAVING AND REVENUES FROM RESOURCE RECOVERY PER TON OF REFUSE TREATED* ($)

REFUSE PROCESSED	AT 500 t.p.d.	AT 1,000 t.p.d.
Net Revenue from sale of products	5.94	7.14
Savings in hauling to landfill	1.00	1.00
Savings in landfill operation	2.00	2.00
Total	8.94	10.14

* No colour sorting of glass. Glass colour sorting by photo electric cells was found to be unprofitable.
SOURCE: US 35.

content of refuse. In fact this figure is likely to considerably overstate the quantity of beverage containers in solid waste because it includes all the other glass and metal items which enter the municipal waste stream. In Section 4 (Table 4.2) the weight of beverage container waste was given as 4 to 6% of all municipal refuse in the USA. Therefore it is unlikely that resource recovery based on the system outlined above will be initiated because of the environmental impact of the beverage container. However, a system such as this will probably alleviate most of the problems referred to in Section 4.b which dealt with the beverage container and solid waste.

5.j.5. Summary

Clearly, there are some potential areas for increased recycling with respect to the beverage container. However, for these schemes to succeed there is a great need for consumers to participate in, and understand, the schemes. Where this voluntary participation can be expected, recycling will provide benefits. However, this participation must be reliable or the economics of such schemes will quickly fail.

Major benefits from recycling will accrue from savings in solid waste management. Unless the recycling rate is high, these benefits are not apparent, because solid waste collection and disposal costs are unlikely to be altered by marginal changes in the quantity of waste. The recycling rate will be determined by the cost of collection of secondary materials; unless this cost is less than the cost of purchasing primary (virgin) materials no private benefit will occur.

Recycling will have no impact on litter. Because of this it is difficult to recommend recycling as a policy to alleviate the external costs of the beverage container, as litter has been identified as a major area of concern. This does not imply that recycling should not be encouraged but merely that it is not a complete solution to all the issues addressed in this report.

5.k.   Technological gains and product innovation

Throughout the analysis so far we have only considered the relative position of the alternative beverage container systems as they stand at present. However, in the beverage industry there is continual research and development into improvements in container design and production processes which will improve the performance of the container, in terms of lowering internal and coincidently external costs. Improvements in transportation, filling and container manufacturing processes, and the development of lighter and alternative containers, would lead to considerable savings in terms of energy consumption, and could also have a beneficial impact on solid waste generation and pollution. RTI estimate that technological advance will result in the annual percentage reductions in the containers' energy requirements shown in Table 5.20, and that these technological changes will result in reductions in the 1985 total systems energy requirements for beer and soft drinks by 28% (US 2).

Incpen (UK 8) and EPA (US 1, JS 6) show that beneficial impacts on solid waste, energy and pollution will result from: modifications in container design; reductions in container weight; the development of new containers such as the all steel beer can and the use of plastic (ABS and PVC) bottles and plastic (PS) - coated glass bottles instead of the non-returnable glass bottles. The gains are especially large if the plastic bottle is refillable as in the case of the Canadian plastic 1/2 gal. milk jug.

However, we found earlier that litter was one of the most important external cost imposed by the beverage containers and such technological developments would not have a marked impact on litter, although the development of plastic coated glass and cans with non-detachable rings pulls will ease the litter problems of discarded ring pulls and broken glass. The development of biodegradable plastics has been advocated on the grounds that it would help solve the problem of accumulated plastic litter. However, this development has many substantial problems, one of which is that it may lead to a greater littering of plastic containers by people who feel that it does not now matter to discard plastics since they will now 'just fade away'.

The RTI estimates, in Table 5.20 show the energy savings to be greater for the metal cans than for the returnable and non-returnable glass bottles and therefore the differential in energy requirements, shown in Section 4.f, could be expected to decline over time.

These energy savings will be the result of energy conservation measures in the beverage industry which are induced by the rise in the internal market price of energy and therefore this represents the policy 'off' situation of no government intervention.

Table 5.20. PROJECTED SAVINGS IN PER-UNIT ENERGY REQUIREMENTS

CONTAINER	ANNUAL SAVINGS %
Returnable glass bottle	
Beer	1.99-2.08
Soft Drinks	1.87
Non-returnable glass bottle	
Beer	2.12
Soft Drinks	2.01
Metal Cans	
Steel	4.03
Aluminium	3.06

SOURCE: US 2.

It has been argued that government intervention in the beverage container market will mean that the market shares of non-returnable containers will fall so that the beverage industry will not now invest in the research and development required to develop new designs, reduce energy and raw materials requirements, and improve efficiencies. However, the allocation of research and development expenditures is determined, among other things, by the expected profitability of the product and one of the principal reasons for the lower level of technological developments in the returnable system in recent years, and in the RTI forecast above, has been the snowballing effect of the returnable bottle's falling market share. Therefore, if the policy measure led to an increase in the profitability and market shares of returnables, then research and development could be expected to improve the returnable system by developing a more durable bottle with a more convenient packaging, which will raise trippage, and by improving process efficiencies in the filling, delivery, retailing and return stages, where there is considerable potential for successful developments.

Also some of the technological advances, which reduce the external costs of the non-returnable containers, will be directly related to the beverage container policy. Thus the Oregon Bottle Bill and public concern over discarded ring pulls have played a major part in encouraging the development of a metal can with a non-detachable ring pull.

Therefore the beverage consumer will still receive benefits from the beverage industry research and development in both the policy 'on' and policy 'off' situations. They will only receive less benefits if the policy leads to a decline in the long run profits level of the total beverage industry, which was one of the economic impact criteria considered in Section 5.a, or if the potential for technological advance is less for the returnable system than for the non-returnable containers.

Appendix 1

FORMULAE FOR THE DERIVATION AND CALCULATION OF TOTAL AND 'OFF' PREMISE TRIPPAGE

Two similar methods (UK 1, SWE 5) have been developed for calculating total trippage (T_T). These require knowledge of:

1. U_b = Sales volume in returnable bottles

2. N = N° of incremental new returnable bottles bought to replace losses in the period. In order to convert this quantity into the same unit as the numerator (sales volume in litres, gals. etc.), it is necessary to multiply it by:

3. AVg size = The average size (in litres, gals. etc.) of returnable bottles.

Thus
$$T_T = \frac{U_b}{N \times \text{AVg size}}$$

The Swedish method (SWE 5) also calculates consumer trippage (Tc) by deducting the figure for in-plant breakages from N to yield the number of bottles that the consumers have failed to return (N con). Thus the consumer trippage (Tc) is given by:

$$T_c = \frac{U_b}{N \text{ con} \times \text{AVg size}}$$

These methods will yield accurate figures for trippage unless the number (N) of new returnable bottles bought in the period does not equal the number of returnables lost in that period. This may occur when there is a sharp increase in total beverage sales or a shift in container mix in favour of returnable which will require an increase in the float of returnable bottles. It is difficult to estimate trippage accurately in these circumstances and care needs to be taken in interpreting the trippage figures in these cases.

'Off' premise trippage (T_T 'off') can be derived by the use of the formula:

$$T_T \text{ 'off'} = \frac{1}{1 - (\text{ARR}_{OFF} - \text{APB}_{OFF})}$$

The inplant breakage rate for 'off' premise returnables (APB_{OFF}) can be expected to be similar or not significantly greater than the breakage rate for 'on' premise sales so that it is reasonable to use the total inplant breakage rate (APB) of about 2%. However, the estimation of the return rate for 'off' premise sales (ARR_{OFF}) is more difficult since it will differ significantly from the 'on' premise return rate and there is a lack of information as to the actual size of the 'off' premise return rate (ARR_{OFF}). One possible method to overcome this problem is to use the formula given below:

$$ARR = \frac{a \cdot ARR_{OFF} + b \cdot ARR_{ON}}{a + b} \quad \text{(CAN 1)}$$

where

ARR = Average return rate for all beverage sales

ARR_{OFF} = Average return rate for 'OFF' premise sales

ARR_{ON} = Average return rate for 'ON' premise sales

a = proportion of returnable beverage sales made to 'OFF' premise customers

b = proportion of returnable beverage sales made to 'ON' premise customers

The calculation of the 'OFF' premise return rate (ARR_{OFF}) requires estimation of the total return (ARR), the 'on' premise return rate, and the proportion of returnable sales made to 'ON' and 'OFF' premise customers. This 'roundabout' method of calculating 'off' premise trippage is used since it is generally easier to obtain data on these four variables than to directly obtain an accurate estimate of the 'off' premise return rate.

The method for calculating the total return rate will yield a fairly accurate result as long as the conditions outlined above hold. Information is more readily available from the more organised and stable 'on' premise market than the dispersed 'off' premise sales market; but even so there is at present a shortage of authoritative data on these four variables and the current estimates of 'on' premise return rates are frequently based more on informed opinion than actual hard data.

The Swedish study (SWE 5) shows that 'on' premise consumption (home delivery, pubs, restaurants, etc.) accounted for 35% of the total beer and soft drink sales in Sweden in 1972. It assumes that the "overwhelming proportion of these 'on' premise sales are in returnables with a return rate of 97.5% (consumer trippage of 40) and that 'on' premise consumption accounts for slightly more than 50% of total returnable sales. It then uses these values to break down the total return rate (ARR) of 96%* into an 'off' premise return rate (ARR$_{OFF}$) of 87.5% which, when combined with an inplant breakage rate of 2%, yields an 'off' premise trippage of 7. However, the accuracy of this figure depends upon the accuracy of the Swedish study's assumptions and values for these variables. This study does not say what it means by 'an overwhelming proportion' but closer examination of other Swedish data (SWE 6) reveals that, in 1972, the proportion of returnable sales to 'on' and 'off' premise customers were 55% and 45% respectively. This enables a calculation of the 'off' premise return rate and trippage as follows:

$$0.96 = \frac{0.45 \times ARR_{OFF} + 0.55 \times 0.975}{0.45 + 0.55}$$

$$\longrightarrow ARR_{OFF} = 94.2\%$$

$$\longrightarrow T_T OFF = \frac{1}{1 - (0.942 - 0.02)} = \frac{1}{0.078}$$

$$\longrightarrow \text{'off' premise trippage} = 12.8$$

The difference between the two studies' figures results from the different data bases and assumptions used and suggest that (SWE 5)'s 'overwhelming proportion' means 100% which may be excessive when one considers that some non-returnables may still be used in the 'on' premise outlets. R. Weinberg (US 33) also uses this method to calculate an 'off' premise trippage of 2.9 for beer. This is lower than the Swedish figure on account of the lower total trippage figure for the USA of 14 (see Table 3.4) and Weinberg's assumptions that 85% of returnable beer sales are made in the 'on' premise market which is assumed to have a trippage of 49.

Thus the estimate for 'on' premise trippage will play an important part in determining the 'off' premise trippage figure. It was started earlier that it is probably easier to make a reasonable estimate of 'on' premise trippage since it should be easier to gain information from the 'on' premise sales outlets which are more likely to keep records on return rates. However, at present, data for 'on' premise trippage is very limited indeed. EPA (US 6) gives a figure of 19 for beer but the current trippage of 25 for the UK milk market, based on home delivery by the milk man, suggests that the actual 'on' premise trippage would be greater than 19 for most countries.

* The total return rate (ARR) of 96% yields a consumer trippage Tc figure of 25 which, when combined with the inplant breakage rate of 2% gives the total trippage figure of 17 given in Table 3.4.

In the light of the lack of data for 'on' premise trippage, an alternative approach is to attempt a direct estimation of 'off' premise trippage by the use of surveys of consumer opinion on their return rates. The Canadian study (CAN 1) quotes one survey which shows that 82% of people, who purchased returnables, returned the bottle; and another survey showed that the rate of returning bottles to the supermarket was 92.4% for customers who usually bought returnables, while only 56.4% for customers who most commonly bought non-returnables. Allowing for the Canadian breakage rate of 1% (CAN 1), this yields a total 'off' premise trippage of 5.3-11.6 for returnable purchasers and 2.2-2.7 for non-returnable purchasers. However, the use of these survey results is suspect for two reasons. First, the telephone replies of the consumers may not equal true return rates due to lack of information on their return rates and the feeling that a 90% return rate is perfect and not much different from 100% when in fact differences in return rates in this range have a marked impact on trippage. Second to be relevant the return rates given by each respondent should be weighted by that respondent's purchases of returnables. As far as we could see this was not done.

If data to undertake the Swedish type calculation is not available, then it is better to use industry estimates. EPA (US 6) quotes industry estimates of 10 for soft drinks and less than 5 for beer 'off' premise trippage. Metal Box (UK 17) undertook a pilot survey of retailers which gives an 'off' premise trippage of between 1.7 and 5 with an average of 3, but they also say that their replies mentioned the lack of knowledge and uncertainty over the required data and "we would not want to attach too much importance to this pilot survey but suggest it might be an approach worth following up".

Thus it is generally agreed that the 'off' premise trippage is lower than the total trippage but there is a lack of agreement and data on the actual size. The data we gathered shows estimates for soft drinks and beer varying from 3 to 13 (ignoring the Canadian surveys) with an average of about 6, which exceeds the breakeven trippage for the returnable bottle in comparison with the alternative containers for energy, and with the non-returnable bottle, but not the metal can, for solid waste (see Table 3.3). However, without more concrete data this remains a tentative conclusion and obviously the 'off' premise trippage will take on different values for each country depending on their different values for total trippage, 'on' premise trippage, and the proportion of returnable sales in 'on' and 'off' premise consumption. The countries' concerned should attempt to make the difficult but important calculations required to derive their own estimates for these parameters, and then use the formulae given here to see if the resulting 'off' premise trippage exceeds the breakeven trippage.

Appendix 2

THE ROLE OF THE VOLUNTARY CO-OPERATION BY INDUSTRY TO INCREASE THE MARKET SHARE OF RETURNABLES

Various delegates raised the question of the extent to which voluntary co-operation by industries, as an alternative to restrictive government legislation, could be relied upon to improve the market position of the returnable bottle and reduce the adverse environmental impact of beverage containers. The benefit of this voluntary approach is that it enables the industries concerned to put their own house in order in the light of various environmental constraints. It is advocated (CAN 5) that the industries' greater knowledge of the workings of the beverage distribution system will result in the formulation of a programme which may achieve the desired environmental improvements while incurring lower economic dislocation impacts on the beverage industry.

However, as was shown in Section 4, it should be noted that the operation of free market forces, will fail by definition to take into account these environmental impacts for external costs of beverage containers, so that there would be no economic incentive to voluntarily reduce the level of these external costs. Therefore in such free market conditions, voluntary co-operation will not on its own achieve the environmental improvements that may be considered desirable. There may be an exception to this in the case where collective action (e.g. by bottlers), designed to improve the internal efficiency of the returnable system or to protect vested interests may also result in environmental improvements. This aspect will be considered later. Nevertheless for most countries the 'voluntary' co-operation that has been achieved is more voluntary in name than nature. Such co-operation has usually been achieved under the threat that if the industry fails to achieve a voluntary solution to the problem, then the government will impose its own restrictive solution on the lines of one of the policy measures considered in Sections 5.c-5.i. An assessment will now be made of four countries experience with voluntary co-operation which will effectively highlight the mandatory nature of such co-operation.

The Danish government passed enabling legislation, in 1970, which gave it powers to introduce a ban on cans. Following this the breweries have, since 1973, made voluntary agreement limiting the quantity of beer sold in cans. These agreements have successfully achieved gradual reduction in canned beer and the eventual elimination of the can is envisaged in 1982. It has been suggested however that a motive behind this action was the desire of the major Danish brewers, who use returnable bottles, to restrict the competition from brewers using cans. The German solid waste management programme recommended that if lightweighting, recycling and other measures did not present an increase in the quantity of glass in solid waste, then the government would consider making restrictive action against the non-returnable containers. This threat was one of the factors behind the expansion in the glass recycling schemes in Germany, which in 1976, yielded 260,000 tons of cullet. This represents 16% of the total glass containers available in the solid waste stream. The success of these schemes were considered separately in the recycling section (5.j) and will not be dealt with in any further detail here.

Further voluntary activity has occured in the German beer markets. In an attempt to improve the systems of returning bottles, the German brewers agreed that each brewer would voluntarily accept beer bottles from retailers for redemption of deposit, irrespective of whether the bottle originated from them. The widespread use of the standard Eurobottle facilitated this system which worked well in Westphalia where there are a small number of brewers. However, in other parts of the country (e.g. Bavaria), where there are a large number of small brewers, the voluntary co-operation has failed. This has resulted in the German brewers asking the government to mandatorily require that all brewers must accept any bottle from a retailer for the redemption of a uniform deposit.

Similarly, in Norway a voluntary deposit system was operated with success by the beer and soft drink producers. However, a few producers did not co-operate with this voluntary system and this resulted in the Norwegian passing legislation which imposed a uniform deposit (NOR 1).

In 1975, the Ontario government announced the objective of its beverage containers policy. These principally were to secure substantial increases in the use of returnable bottles and to undertake measures (e.g. standardization) to improve the efficiency of a returnable system. The benefits of industrial co-operation in securing these objectives was recognized and a directive was issued to the soft drink manufactures and retailers that, if these objectives could not be achieved through their voluntary action, then the government would step in an implement legislative action. The industries concerned were then given 12 months in which to formulate a voluntary programme and demonstrate its effectiveness. This voluntary action resulted in an agreement on some form of standardization and an undertaking by the retailers to improve the marketing position of returnable bottles (e.g. by increasing the availability of soft drinks in returnable bottles and showing separately the price of the beverage from the deposit on the bottle). It was agreed to increase the promotional advertising for the returnable bottle and a task force was set up to consider how to increase the efficiency of the distribution and return processes for the returnables.

In 1976, at the end of the 12 months period, the position was reviewed by the government advisory board which expressed that, although some progress had been made, it was generally disappointed with the response and progress of industry in securing the government's objectives. Specifically the board found that during 1975, the market shares of the returnable bottle had increased, reversing the trend of previous years towards non-returnables, and that there had been a slight increase in the availability in shops of soft drinks in returnable bottles, although this increase was only six percentage points. The board discovered that considerable problems were involved in co-ordinating the multitude of diverse and independent bodies in the soft drink manufacturing and retailing sectors. There was a considerable delay before these parties could come to a common agreement and then it was difficult to ensure that this agreement was adhered to by all parties. Thus independent retailers still continued to move towards non-returnable and it was not possible to obtain uniform support for a standardization programme. This dissatisfaction with the effectiveness of voluntary control led the advisory board to decide that voluntary co-operation, on its own, was inadequate and that therefore direct government intervention was now required.

In conclusion therefore it can be seen that benefits can be gained from securing the voluntary co-operation of industry, whose knowledge of the beverage distribution system will aid the formulation of a policy with less dislocation impacts on the industry. However the disadvantage of voluntary control creates doubts as to whether it can be relied upon in some circumstances to secure the desired level of environmental improvement. The threat of direct governement action can probably create conditions which encourage the beverage industry to internalize the external costs of beverage containers. The experience of the four countries, analyzed above, suggest that such 'voluntary' action is more likely to be effective where there is an organized beverage market containing a small number of bottlers (e.g. the Danish and Westphalian German beer markets) than in dispersed beverage markets such as the Bavarian beer market and Ontario soft drink market where government action would appear to be a more appropriate method of achieving the desired level of environmental improvement.

Appendix 3

REFERENCES

Australia

(AUS 1)　　Report on Deposits on Beverage Containers, House of Representatives Standing Committee on Environment and Conservation, 1974. Parliamentary Paper No. 273.

(AUS 2)　　Submission of comments by Australian delegation to OECD Waste Management Policy Group.

Canada

(CAN 1)　　An Environmental Study of Beverage Packaging. Solid Waste Task Force. General Report to the Ontario Minister of the Environment, 1974. (2 vols.).

(CAN 2)　　Lets Keep our Regional Economy, Quebec Soft Drink Bottlers Association, October 1972.

(CAN 3)　　Burlington Waste Reclamation Pilot Study. Final Report, 1972. Prepared for the waste management branch of the Ontario Ministry of the Environment by Philips Planning and Engineering Ltd, Burlington.

(CAN 4)　　The Carbonated soft drink container in Ontario. Report of the Waste Management Advisory Board. Ministry of the Environment, March 1976.

(CAN 5)　　Joint submission by Retail Council of Canada and the Ontario Soft Drink Association to the Minister of the Environment, Province of Ontario.

Denmark

(DK 1)　　Submission by Danish Delegation to OECD Waste Management Policy Group.

Finland

(FIN 1)　　Submission by Finnish Delegation to the OECD Waste Management Policy Group.

France

(FR 1) F. Pardos - Jacques, Comparaisons Internationales des Industries de l'Emballage, Emballages, December 1974.

(FR 2) E. Suzanne (ed.), Proposition d'actions visant à réduire les dépenses d'énergie dans le conditionnement des produits alimentaires, PMM and Co., Consultants, COFRAT Groupe MATRA.

(FR 3) Les Déchets solides : proposition pour une politique - Rapport du groupe d'études sur l'élimination des résidus solides.

(FR 4) Les résidus de l'industrie du verre: A. Richard. September, 1974.

Germany

(FRG 1) Abfallwirtschaftsprogramm 1975 der Bundesregierung.- Der Bundesminister des Innern, U II 6-530 021/1.

(FRG 2) Battelle Institut e. V. Frankfurt, Untersuchung uber die Moglichen Auswirkungen einer Ausgleichsabgabe auf Einwegflaschen aus Glas bzw. eines Verbotes, 1975.

(FRG 3) Comments from German delegate to the Waste Management Policy Group.

(FRG 4) 'Glass recycling in Germany - the actual situation' G. Lubish, Glass, vol. 54, No. 4 April 1977.

Japan

(JAP 1) Case Study of Re-Use and Recycling of Beverage Containers, especially prepared for OECD, 1975.

Netherlands

(NETH 1) Instituut TNO voor Verpakking - Mono of Retourverpakking, Delft, February, 1975.

(NETH 2) Instituut TNO voor Verpakking - Consequenties van Afvalverpakkingen voor Milieu en Vuilverwerking, Deel I : Melkverpakking, Delft, August, 1974.

(NETH 3) Stichting Verwijdering Afvalstoffen, Hergebruik Verpakkingsglas, Amersfoort, June 1974.

(NETH 4)   Stichting Verpakking en Milieu. - <u>Een Methode voor Vergelijkend Onderzoek van Verpakkingssystemen</u>, March 1976.

(NETH 5)   <u>Recovery of Glass in Europe</u>. Ir. J.A. van der Kuil., December, 1974.

(NETH 6)   Submission of comments by Dutch delegation to Waste Management Policy Group. OECD.

(NETH 7)   <u>Case Study on Packaging</u>. W.P. Fornerod - Paper submitted to an ECE Seminar, December 1976.

(NETH 8)   Stichting Verwijdering Afvalstoffen. - <u>Terugwinning Verpakkingsblik</u>, November 1975.

(NETH 9)   <u>Recovery of Materials by Separate Collection of Domestic Waste Components</u>. J.A. van der Kuil. Institute for Waste Disposal, Amersfoort.

(NETH 10) Submission of comments by Secretariat of Dutch Packaging Institute.

Norway

(NOR 1)   Submission of comments by Norwegian Delegation to OECD Waste Management Policy Group.

Sweden

(SWE 1)   I. Olsson, <u>Duty on Beverage Containers in Sweden</u>, National Swedish Environment Protection Board, 1975.

(SWE 2)   Effekter av Forpackningsavgiften, SOU, 1974.

(SWE 3)   G. Sundstrom. <u>Dryckesforpackningarna och Energin</u>, (no date).

(SWE 4)   <u>Dryckesforpackningar och miljo</u>. Betankande av utredningen om Kostnaderna for Miljovarden. SOU, 1976.

(SWE 5)   Karl Lidgren. <u>Containers and Environmental Policy</u>, 1976.

(SWE 6)   <u>The Beverage Market in Sweden, 1973, 1974 and 1975</u>. PLM Metal Division and Glass Division.

(SWE 7)   Households Contributing to Resource Recovery. A survey published by the Swedish Institute for Resource Recovery.

Switzerland

(SWI 1) Basler und Hofman, Studie Unwelt und Volkwirtschaft-Vergleich der Unweltbelastung von Behaltern aus PVC, Glass. Blech und Karton, 1974. Prepared for Swiss Federal Office for the Protection of the Environment.

(SWI 2) F. Emch, Studie über die Möglichkeiten und Grenzen der Anwendung gleicher Flaschen für Lebensmittelflüssigkeiten, 1975. Prepared for the Swiss Federal Office for the Protection of the Environment.

(SWI 3) Institut du génie de l'environnement. Récupération du verre : Rapport Final, Prepared for Swiss Federal Office for the Protection of the Environment.

(SWI 4) Mehrwegglas, Einwegglas, Altglasverwertung, Eidgenossiches Amt. für Umweltschutz, April 1976.

(SWI 5) Submission of comments by Swiss Delegation to Waste Management Policy Group. OECD.

(SWI 6) Pr. V. Maystre. 'The application of systems analysis to environmental Engineering. A multi-objective uncertain case of application : Bottles and/or cullet recycling of glass in Switzerland. Lausanne, 1976.

United Kingdom

(UK 1) S. Spence and D.W. Pearce, The Social Costs and Benefits of Packaging with Special Reference to Returnable and Non-Returnable Carbonated Drinks Containers, 1975. Prepared for the Department of the Environment.

(UK 2) Plastics Waste Disposal : Some Important Considerations. Final Report of the Working Party on Designing for Disposability. The Plastics Institute, January 1974.

(UK 3) Wine and Spirit Bottle Recovery. Pilot Feasibility Study. P.E. Consulting Group Ltd, June 1974.

(UK 4) The Glass Container Industry and the Environmental Debate. Glass Manufacturers Federation, November, 1973.

(UK 5) Glass Container Recovery: its viability. Redfearn National Glass Limited, June 1974.

(UK 6) Plastics Waste and Litter. J.J.P. Staudinger. Society of Chemical Industry, 1970.

(UK 7) Metal Containers and the Environment. Metal Box Co. Ltd.

(UK 8) Packaging and the Energy Equation. Incpen (Industry Committee for Packaging and the Environment), Discussion Paper No. 3.

(UK 9) Improving the Quality of Life - Through Better Packaging. Incpen (Industry Committee for Packaging and the Environment) Discussion Paper No. 1, April 1975.

(UK 10) Refuse Disposal and Packaging. Incpen Discussion Paper No. 6.

(UK 11) Comments by Metal Box on Peaker's paper on the Oregon Bottle Law (US 4).

(UK 12) Comments by Metal Box Ltd. on behalf of the British Tin Box Manufacturers Federation.

(UK 13) 'Resource implications with particular reference to energy requirements for glass and plastic milk bottles'. I. Boustead. Journal of Society of Dairy Technology, Vol. 27, No. 3, July 1974.

(UK 14) In Defence of Economic Growth - W. Beckerman, 1974.

(UK 15) The limits to Growth. A report for the Club of Rome's project on the predicament of mankind. D.H. and D.L. Meadows, J. Randers and W.W. Behrens III, 1972.

(UK 16) The Desirability of natural resource depletion. J. Kay and J. Mirrlees in 'Economics of Natural Resource Depletion', edited by D.W. Pearce.

(UK 17) Data and information supplied by Metal Box Market Research Division.

(UK 18) Trippage of Returnable Soft Drink Bottles. National Association of Soft Drink Manufacturers Limited. September, 1976.

(UK 19) Submission of data by National Soft Drinks Manufacturers Association.

(UK 20)   'The Economics of Energy Analysis'. M. Webb and D.W. Pearce, Energy Policy, December 1975.

(UK 21)   Data obtained in correspondence with United Glass Containers Ltd.

(UK 22)   Submission of comments by UK delegation to OECD Waste Management Policy Group.

(UK 23)   Presentation to the Packaging and Container Working Group of UK Waste Management Advisory Council (WMAC) by United Glass.

(UK 24)   Recycling of Tinplate Containers. A joint study undertaken by K. Dudley (Metal Bix Co. Ltd.), B. Lindley (Batchelor Robinson Co. Ltd.) and W. Laws (British Steel Corporation), November 1974.

(UK 25)   Correspondence with Schweppes Ltd. (UK).

(UK 26)   'The concept of over-packaging' Submission by the Department of the Environment to the Packaging and Containers Working Group of the UK Waste Management Advisory Council.

(UK 27)   Submission of comments by Friends of the Earth.

(UK 28)   'Energy studies relating to glass containers' Glass Manufacturers Federation.

(UK 29)   'Energy conservation'. A study by the Central Policy Review Staff. HMSO, 1975.

(UK 30)   'Material Gains - Reclamation, Recycling and Re-Use', C. Thomas, Friends of the Earth, Ltd., 1974.

(UK 31)   Submission of comments by UK delegation to OECD Waste Management Policy Group.

(UK 32)   The Brewers Society, Statistical Handbook, 1976.

(UK 33)   'Oxfam Wastesaver. An analysis of the operating costs: March-May, 1976'. A. Forbes. September 1976.

(UK 34)   'Many Happy returns. Glass containers and the Environment.' R. Bate, Friends of the Earth, 1976.

(UK 35)   'Glass Recycling in Europe'. Glass Manufacturers Federation.

(UK 36)   'Oxfam Wastesaver scheme enters third year'. Materials Reclamation Weekly, March 5th, 1977.

United States

(US 1)   US Environmental Protection Agency, Resources Recovery and Waste Reduction, Third Report to Congress, 1975.

(US 2)   Research Triangle Institute, Energy and Economic Impacts of Mandatory Deposits, 1975. Prepared for the US Federal Energy Administration.

(US 3)   US Environmental Protection Agency, The Beverage Container Problem, 1972.

(US 4)   A. Peaker, Environmental Effects and an Assessment of Legislation in the State of Oregon Requiring that all Beer and Carbonated Soft Drink Containers be Returnable Against a Deposit, 1975.

(US 5)   Research Triangle Institute, An Evaluation of the Effectiveness and Costs of Regulatory and Fiscal Policy Instruments on Product Packaging. Final Report, 1974. Prepared for the Environmental Protection Agency.

(US 6)   U.S. Environmental Protection Agency. Resource and Environmental Profile Analysis of Nine Beverage Container Alternatives, 1974.

(US 7)   Glass Recycling and Re-Use. Harold R. Samtur. Institute for Environmental Studies University of Wisconsin, 1974.

(US 8)   System Energy and Recycling. A study of the Beverage Industry. Bruce Hannon. Centre for Advanced Computation. University of Illinois, 1973.

(US 9)   The National Economic Impact of a Ban on Non-Refillable Beverage Containers. Midwest Research Institute, 1971.

(US 10)   Report on Litter Management in California. State Solid Waste Management Board, December, 1974.

(US 11)   Two Papers on the Effects of Mandatory Deposits on Beverage Containers. Hugh Folk. Centre for Advanced Computation. University of Illinois, 1975.

(US 12)   The Soft Drink Industry. Research Triangle Institute 1976.

(US 13)   The Brewing Industry. Research Triangle Institute, 1976.

(US 14)   Beverage Container Regulation, Economic Implications and Suggestions for Model Legislation. Charles Gudger and Kenneth Walters. Stanford Ecology Law Quarterly. Vol. 5, 1976.

(US 15)   The Economic Impact of Oregons' "Bottle Bill". Gudger and Bailes. Oregon U.P., 1974.

(US 16)   Impacts of National Beverage Container Legislation. Bureau of Domestic Commerce. US Dept. of Commerce, 1975.

(US 17)   Impacts of Beverage Container Legislation on Connecticut and a Review of the Experience of Oregon, Vermont and Washington State.
C. Stern, E. Verdieck, S. Smith and T. Hedrick. University of Connecticut, Storrs, March 1975.

(US 18)   Impacts of Beverage Container Regulations in Minnesota. Minnesota State Planning Agency, 1974, quoted in (US 17).

(US 19)   Report to the Governor of Vermont from Governor's Highway Litter Evaluation Committee. December 1973.

(US 20)   Statement of J.R. Quarles, Deputy Administrator, Environmental Protection Agency, before the subcommittee on the environment Senate committee on commerce. United States Senate, May 1974.

(US 21)   Consumer Protection II - Oregon Department of Agriculture, December 1973.

(US 22)   The Economic Impact of a Proposed Mandatory Deposit on beer and soft drink containers in California. Legislative Analyst, State of California, October 1975.

(US 23)   US Environmental Protection Agency. Fourth Report to Congress, 1977.

(US 24)   A Report on Litter in the State of Washington Pursuant to the Model Litter Control Act. URS Company, prepared for Department of Ecology, Washington, June 1975.

(US 25) The Structure of the US Economy in 1980 and 1985. US Department of Labour, Bureau of Labour Statistics, 1975.

(US 26) The Effect of Convenience Packaging in the Malt Beverage Industry 1947-1969. RS Weinberg and Associates, 1971.

(US 27) No Deposit, No Return. New York State Task Force on Critical Problems. February 1975.

(US 28) Disposing of Non-Returnables. E.F. Lowry et. al., Stanford Environmental Law Society, 1975.

(US 29) A Summary Evaluation of the Environmental Impacts of Beverage Container Systems. Stanford Research Institute. Merlo Park, California, 1974.

(US 30) Study of the Effectiveness and Impact of the Oregon Minimum Deposit Law. Applied Decisions Systems, 1974.

(US 31) Statement of Sidney P. Mudd, President, National Soft Drink Association, before sub-committee on transportation and commerce committee on interstate and foreign commerce. US House of Representatives, Washington D.C. 1975.

(US 32) US Environmental Protection Agency. Second Report to Congress, 1974.

(US 33) Comments on RTI's first draft report of energy and economic impacts of mandatory deposits.

(US 34) The Status of Non-Waste Technology in the UK Packaging Industry. W.D. Conn, August, 1976.

(US 35) Bureau of Mines Process for Recovering Resources from Raw Refuse. P.M. Sullivan, H.V. Makar; a paper in the Proceedings of the Fourth Mineral Waste Utilization Symposium (1974).

(US 36) Testimony of P.A. Korody, Director of Governmental affairs, National association of food chains, on S. 2062, Non-returnable beverage container prohibition Act, before the committee on commerce, U.S. Senate, May 1974.

(US 37) Statement by R.L. Johnson, National Association of retail grocers of the United States, before the subcommittee on the Environmental Senate committee on commerce, May 1974.

(US 38) Social costs of beverage containers. An economic analysis of six legislative solutions for Maryland. J.J. Tawil, Division of Research, the Department of Economic and Community Development, Maryland, March 1976.

European Communities

(EEC 1) Collecte, Elimination et Recyclage des emballages non biodegradables. Commission des Communautés Européennes, 1974 (2 vols.). ENV/135/76.

(EEC 2) L'évolution de la concentration dans l'industrie de la brasserie en France. Commission des Communautés Européennes, 1975.

(EEC 3) 'Combined Statistics' Communauté de Travail des Brasseurs du Marché Commun (CBMC)/EFTA Brewing Industry Council (EBIC), 1975.

(EEC 4) 'Non-alcoholic and alcoholic beverages in Italy' and 'Non-alcoholic and alcoholic beverages in France'. Marketing in Europe, January, 1977.

Appendix 4

RECOMMENDATION OF THE COUNCIL CONCERNING THE RE-USE AND RECYCLING OF BEVERAGE CONTAINERS

(Adopted by the OECD Council on 3rd February, 1978)

The Council,

Having regard to Article 5(b) of the Convention on the Organisation for Economic Co-operation and Development of 14th December, 1960;

Having regard to the Recommendation of the Council of 28th September, 1976 on a Comprehensive Waste Management Policy, calling in particular for the development and implementation of measures to reduce waste generation and encourage recycling;

Considering that beverage containers do not account for an insignificant proportion of household waste and are a major source of litter; and that clean-up and disposal costs are a matter of concern to local authorities and governments in many Member countries;

Considering that in many countries the generally observed trend in the beverage container market is towards the replacement of refillable bottles by disposable containers, thus tending to make problems of waste disposal more acute;

Considering that systems of beverage distribution by refillable containers, over and above a certain trippage which is generally achieved in practice, are at present proving superior to most other systems not only as concerns municipal solid waste generation but also from such standpoints as energy consumption, litter, air and water pollution;

Considering that certain measures such as the standardization of containers and the recycling of their constituent materials can also greatly help to reduce waste disposal problems, either by encouraging the introduction and satisfactory operation of a system of refillable containers, or by refillable containers, or by creating conditions likely to divert certain forms of waste from the disposal circuit with a view to their profitable reclamation;

Considering that national policies towards the internalisation of external costs are to be implemented on the basis of action principles common to all Member countries, in order to avoir the creation of trade barriers;

Having regard to the Report of the Environment Committee on the re-use and recycling of beverage containers, where practical measures which can be envisaged for implementing the present Recommendation are discussed in detail;

On the proposal of the Environment Committee;

I. RECOMMENDS that Member countries, through international co-operation as appropriate, where practicable define and implement policies designed to ensure that the costs of the adverse environmental impacts of the manufacture and use of beverage containers are effectively and equitably borne by the producers and users of such containers.

II. RECOMMENDS that Member countries adopt appropriate measures with a view to maintaining, or where necessary introducing, a system of distribution by refillable containers covering as much as possible of the beverage trade when it is expected that, in doing so, the social costs of the beverage distribution systems are minimized.

III. RECOMMENDS that, when measures to promote the use of refillable beverage containers are considered, they be accompanied by an effort to standardize such containers, possibly undertaken on the basis of collaboration between the countries concerned in order to prevent trade barriers.

IV. RECOMMENDS that, regardless of the measures taken to promote the re-use of beverage containers, Member countries encourage the recycling of the ultimately disposed-of containers, and take any other necessary step to reduce as much as possible any adverse effect they may have on the environment.

OECD SALES AGENTS
DÉPOSITAIRES DES PUBLICATIONS DE L'OCDE

ARGENTINA – ARGENTINE
Carlos Hirsch S.R.L., Florida 165,
BUENOS-AIRES, Tel. 33-1787-2391 Y 30-7122

AUSTRALIA – AUSTRALIE
International B.C.N. Library Suppliers Pty Ltd.,
161 Sturt St., South MELBOURNE, Vic. 3205. Tel. 699-6388
P.O.Box 202, COLLAROY, NSW 2097. Tel. 982 4515

AUSTRIA – AUTRICHE
Gerold and Co., Graben 31, WIEN 1. Tel. 52.22.35

BELGIUM – BELGIQUE
Librairie des Sciences,
Coudenberg 76-78, B 1000 BRUXELLES 1. Tel. 512-05-60

BRAZIL – BRÉSIL
Mestre Jou S.A., Rua Guaipà 518,
Caixa Postal 24090, 05089 SAO PAULO 10. Tel. 261-1920
Rua Senador Dantas 19 s/205-6, RIO DE JANEIRO GB.
Tel. 232-07. 32

CANADA
Renouf Publishing Company Limited,
2182 St. Catherine Street West,
MONTREAL, Quebec H3H 1M7 Tel. (514) 937-3519

DENMARK – DANEMARK
Munksgaards Boghandel,
Nørregade 6, 1165 KØBENHAVN K. Tel. (01) 12 69 70

FINLAND – FINLANDE
Akateeminen Kirjakauppa
Keskuskatu 1, 00100 HELSINKI 10. Tel. 625.901

FRANCE
Bureau des Publications de l'OCDE,
2 rue André-Pascal, 75775 PARIS CEDEX 16. Tel. 524.81.67
Principal correspondant :
13602 AIX-EN-PROVENCE : Librairie de l'Université.
Tel. 26.18.08

GERMANY – ALLEMAGNE
Verlag Weltarchiv G.m.b.H.
D 2000 HAMBURG -36, Neuer Jungfernstieg 21.
Tel. 040-35-62-500

GREECE – GRÈCE
Librairie Kauffmann, 28 rue du Stade,
ATHÈNES 132. Tel. 322.21.60

HONG-KONG
Government Information Services,
Sales and Publications Office, Beaconsfield House, 1st floor,
Queen's Road, Central. Tel. H-233191

ICELAND – ISLANDE
Snaebjörn Jönsson and Co., h.f.,
Hafnarstraeti 4 and 9, P.O.B. 1131, REYKJAVIK.
Tel. 13133/14281/11936

INDIA – INDE
Oxford Book and Stationery Co.:
NEW DELHI, Scindia House. Tel. 45896
CALCUTTA, 17 Park Street. Tel.240832

IRELAND - IRLANDE
Eason and Son, 40 Lower O'Connell Street,
P.O.B. 42, DUBLIN 1. Tel. 74 39 35

ISRAËL
Emanuel Brown: 35 Allenby Road, TEL AVIV. Tel. 51049/54082
also at:
9, Shlomzion Hamalka Street, JERUSALEM. Tel. 234807
48, Nahlath Benjamin Street, TEL AVIV. Tel. 53276

ITALY – ITALIE
Libreria Commissionaria Sansoni:
Via Lamarmora 45, 50121 FIRENZE. Tel. 579751
Via Bartolini 29, 20155 MILANO. Tel. 365083
Sub-depositari:
Editrice e Libreria Herder,
Piazza Montecitorio 120, 00 186 ROMA. Tel. 674628
Libreria Hoepli, Via Hoepli 5, 20121 MILANO. Tel. 865446
Libreria Lattes, Via Garibaldi 3, 10122 TORINO. Tel. 519274
La diffusione delle edizioni OCSE è inoltre assicurata dalle migliori
librerie nelle città più importanti.

JAPAN – JAPON
OECD Publications Center,
Akasaka Park Building, 2-3-4 Akasaka, Minato-ku,
TOKYO 107. Tel. 586-2016

KOREA - CORÉE
Pan Korea Book Corporation,
P.O.Box n°101 Kwangwhamun, SÉOUL. Tel. 72-7369

LEBANON – LIBAN
Documenta Scientifica/Redico,
Edison Building, Bliss Street, P.O.Box 5641, BEIRUT.
Tel. 354429–344425

MEXICO & CENTRAL AMERICA
Centro de Publicaciones de Organismos Internacionales S.A.,
Av. Chapultepec 345, Apartado Postal 6-981
MEXICO 6, D.F. Tel. 533-45-09

THE NETHERLANDS – PAYS-BAS
Staatsuitgeverij
Chr. Plantijnstraat
'S-GRAVENHAGE. Tel. 070-814511
Voor bestillingen: Tel. 070-624551

NEW ZEALAND – NOUVELLE-ZÉLANDE
The Publications Manager,
Government Printing Office,
WELLINGTON: Mulgrave Street (Private Bag),
World Trade Centre, Cubacade, Cuba Street,
Rutherford House, Lambton Quay, Tel. 737-320
AUCKLAND: Rutland Street (P.O.Box 5344), Tel. 32.919
CHRISTCHURCH: 130 Oxford Tce (Private Bag), Tel. 50.331
HAMILTON: Barton Street (P.O.Box 857), Tel. 80.103
DUNEDIN: T & G Building, Princes Street (P.O.Box 1104),
Tel. 78.294

NORWAY – NORVÈGE
Johan Grundt Tanums Bokhandel,
Karl Johansgate 41/43, OSLO 1. Tel. 02-332980

PAKISTAN
Mirza Book Agency, 65 Shahrah Quaid-E-Azam, LAHORE 3.
Tel. 66839

PHILIPPINES
R.M. Garcia Publishing House, 903 Quezon Blvd. Ext.,
QUEZON CITY, P.O.Box 1860 – MANILA. Tel. 99.98.47

PORTUGAL
Livraria Portugal, Rua do Carmo 70-74, LISBOA 2. Tel. 360582/3

SPAIN – ESPAGNE
Mundi-Prensa Libros, S.A.
Castelló 37, Apartado 1223, MADRID-1. Tel. 275.46.55
Libreria Bastinos, Pelayo, 52, BARCELONA 1. Tel. 222.06.00

SWEDEN – SUÈDE
AB CE Fritzes Kungl Hovbokhandel,
Box 16 356, S 103 27 STH, Regeringsgatan 12,
DS STOCKHOLM. Tel. 08/23 89 00

SWITZERLAND – SUISSE
Librairie Payot, 6 rue Grenus, 1211 GENÈVE 11. Tel. 022-31.89.50

TAIWAN – FORMOSE
National Book Company,
84-5 Sing Sung Rd., Sec. 3, TAIPEI 107. Tel. 321.0698

UNITED KINGDOM – ROYAUME-UNI
H.M. Stationery Office, P.O.B. 569,
LONDON SEI 9 NH. Tel. 01-928-6977, Ext. 410
or
49 High Holborn, LONDON WC1V 6 HB (personal callers)
Branches at: EDINBURGH, BIRMINGHAM, BRISTOL,
MANCHESTER, CARDIFF, BELFAST.

UNITED STATES OF AMERICA
OECD Publications Center, Suite 1207, 1750 Pennsylvania Ave.,
N.W. WASHINGTON, D.C.20006. Tel.   (202)724-1857

VENEZUELA
Libreria del Este, Avda. F. Miranda 52, Edificio Galipán,
CARACAS 106. Tel. 32 23 01/33 26 04/33 24 73

YUGOSLAVIA – YOUGOSLAVIE
Jugoslovenska Knjiga, Terazije 27, P.O.B. 36, BEOGRAD.
Tel. 621-992

Les commandes provenant de pays où l'OCDE n'a pas encore désigné de dépositaire peuvent être adressées à :
OCDE, Bureau des Publications, 2 rue André-Pascal, 75775 PARIS CEDEX 16.
Orders and inquiries from countries where sales agents have not yet been appointed may be sent to:
OECD, Publications Office, 2 rue André-Pascal, 75775 PARIS CEDEX 16.

OECD PUBLICATIONS, 2, rue André-Pascal, 75775 Paris Cedex 16 - No. 40.217 1978
PRINTED IN FRANCE